A Gift For

From

Date

Life Principles FOR THE Graduate

Nine Truths for Living God's Way

CHARLES F. STANLEY

Life Principles for the Graduate

Published in Nashville, Tennessee, by Thomas Nelson®, Inc.
Thomas Nelson is a registered trademark of Thomas Nelson®, Inc.

Project Editor: Jessica Inman
Project Manager: Lisa Stilwell

Designed by Koechel Peterson & Associates, Inc., Minneapolis, MN

ISBN-10: 1-4041-8698-0
ISBN-13: 978-1-4041-8698-9

Printed and bound in China

www.thomasnelson.com

08 09 10 11 12 [WAI] 6 5 4 3 2 1

Table of Contents

INTRODUCTION

AS YOU APPROACH GRADUATION, you probably are thinking about your future more than ever. You are making decisions that will affect the rest of your life, and you're trying to create the best life possible for yourself. Throughout my life's journey, I have come to understand one thing clearly: only God can help you live a truly extraordinary life.

When you place your hope in temporal things—money, social status, achievements, acceptance, or even the love of your family and friends—your foundation will inevitably crumble. Worldly comforts are no defense against the tumultuous storms that life often delivers. Your identity must be based on something greater than what the world offers if you are to stand strong.

As the old saying goes, life is not about *who* you are; it's about *whose* you are. Being able to answer this one question is extremely important because it has essentially everything to do with your personal relationship with God and your future. Your challenge is to get to know Him and, in the process, get yourself out of the way so He can move in and through you. He has a distinct purpose for your life, and He wants you to understand that purpose. When you finally see how beloved you are and how great your calling is, you will sense a desire growing within you to live for Him through His power.

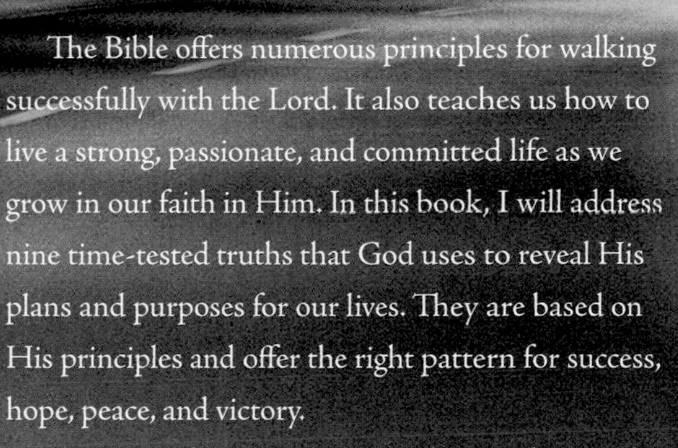

The Bible offers numerous principles for walking successfully with the Lord. It also teaches us how to live a strong, passionate, and committed life as we grow in our faith in Him. In this book, I will address nine time-tested truths that God uses to reveal His plans and purposes for our lives. They are based on His principles and offer the right pattern for success, hope, peace, and victory.

Becoming the masterpiece God created you to be is a lifelong process in which He is continually shaping you into a unique reflection of His Son. It is my prayer that you will embrace each one of these principles fully and, in so doing, discover the extraordinary life God has planned for you.

Charles F. Stanley

SURRENDER: *The Starting Point*

Fulfillment is not a matter of position or power. It is a matter of loving God and allowing Him to love you. All you need in order to be fulfilled is Jesus Christ living within you. So submit yourself to God. Fulfillment comes only when you decide to love God and give Him all of yourself. He has a great plan for your life—a life that is exceptional.

SURRENDER *is the First Step*

For if the readiness is present, it is acceptable according to what a person has, not according to what he does not have.

2 CORINTHIANS 8:12

GOD DESIGNED YOUR LIFE FOR HIS GLORY. Even before you knew Him personally, He knew you intimately: "O LORD, You have searched me and known me. You know when I sit down and when I rise up; you understand my thought from afar. You scrutinize my path and my lying down, and are intimately acquainted with all my ways" (Psalm 139:1–3). When we surrender ourselves to God, we exchange our old thoughts, feelings, and desires for new ones. Faith is the only way we can do this. By faith we believe that God is who He says He is and that He will do exactly what He has promised.

We still can reach our goals, overcome our failures, and enjoy success, but for a different reason. Instead of boasting about what we have achieved in our own capabilities, we can enjoy what God has given abundantly. Our lives become reflections of His life and love rather than a checklist of human accomplishments.

Submit yourself to God. Fulfillment comes only when you decide to love God and give Him all of yourself. This does not mean that you settle for second best or stop doing what you have been trained to do. Instead, you come to a point where you ask God to use you to the fullest so that others will come to know Him and experience His forgiveness and unconditional love. Those who have never discovered the wondrous joy that comes from loving and serving God have yet to experience His eternal fulfillment.

EACH ONE OF US HAS BEEN BLESSED WITH SPIRITUAL GIFTS TO BE USED FOR GOD'S GLORY AND WORK. YIELDING TO HIM IS THE FIRST STEP IN THE PROCESS OF DISCOVERING THOSE GIFTS AND THE WONDROUS PURPOSE FOR YOUR LIFE.

God has a great plan for your life—a life that is exceptional. "'For I know the plans that I have for you,' declares the LORD, 'plans for welfare and not for calamity to give you a future and a hope'" (Jeremiah 29:11). When you trust and seek only Him, He will teach you how to live above your circumstances. Each one of us has been blessed with spiritual gifts to be used for God's glory and work. Yielding to Him is the first step in the process of discovering those gifts and the wondrous purpose for your life.

We Can Rely on GOD'S GREAT LOVE

We have come to know and have believed the love which God has for us. God is love, and the one who abides in love abides in God, and God abides in him. There is no fear in love; but perfect love casts out fear, because fear involves punishment, and the one who fears is not perfected in love.

I JOHN 4:16, 18

SO OFTEN WE RUN FROM GOD, thinking we need to escape His punishment or avoid doing some task He wants us to do. But what we are actually doing is eluding His will and best for us.

God is omniscient. He knows all about us. He knows what we have done in the past and what we will do in the future. The wondrous thing about His love is that it never stops. He loves us the same today as He did yesterday, and His love for us will never change. When we feel as though we have failed in life, He comes to us and raises up a banner of hope on our behalf: "Hope does not disappoint, because the love of God has been poured out within our hearts through the Holy Spirit who was given to us" (Romans 5:5).

You may wonder why it is so difficult to live the Christian life. Why do so many people end up living less-than-productive lives? The answers to these questions are found in our ability to accept and apply a crucial truth to our hearts: it is God's unconditional love that changes us and brings lasting fulfillment. Once we understand and accept that there is no greater

love than the love of God, we will be ready to take the first step toward living the life He has planned for us.

What goals do you hope to achieve? What dreams has God placed within your heart—ones that you long to see become realities? Despite your fears and insecurities, you can achieve the goals He has given. There is a way to live each day fulfilled, satisfied, and blessed. He is the One who gives us many of the desires we have.

God created you in the image of His Son, the Lord Jesus Christ, and as a believer, His power exists within you. Surrendering to His will and purpose is one of the first steps in achieving a life of fulfillment. Once you begin your journey into His blessings, you will never want to turn back. The world may promise fame, fortune, and material possessions, but it does not deliver. There is a huge, deadly cost involved whenever you go against God's best. Instead of falling prey to sin and failure, make a decision to stand firm in your faith by trusting Him to guide you in a direction that will lead to unimaginable blessings.

WE HAVE TO ACCEPT AND APPLY A CRUCIAL TRUTH TO OUR HEARTS: IT IS GOD'S UNCONDITIONAL LOVE THAT CHANGES US AND BRINGS LASTING FULFILLMENT.

ABIDING *in Christ*

But, indeed, for this reason I have allowed you to remain, in order to show you My power and in order to proclaim My name through all the earth.

EXODUS 9:16

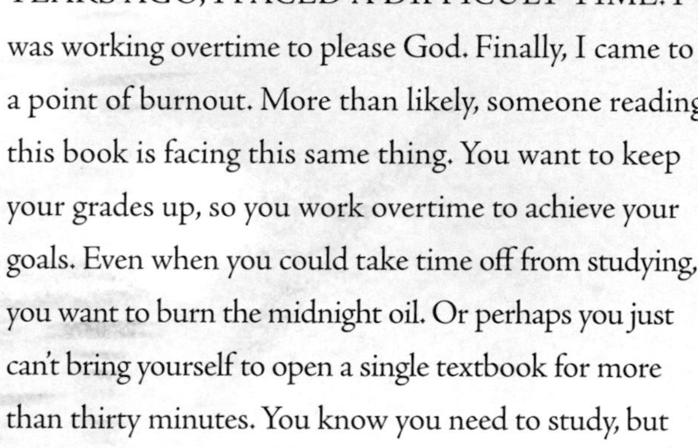

YEARS AGO, I FACED A DIFFICULT TIME. I was working overtime to please God. Finally, I came to a point of burnout. More than likely, someone reading this book is facing this same thing. You want to keep your grades up, so you work overtime to achieve your goals. Even when you could take time off from studying, you want to burn the midnight oil. Or perhaps you just can't bring yourself to open a single textbook for more than thirty minutes. You know you need to study, but your mind keeps drifting.

God ministered to me through John 15: "Abide in Me, and I in you. . . . I am the vine, you are the branches; he who abides in Me and I in him, he bears much fruit, for apart from Me you can do nothing" (vv. 4–5).

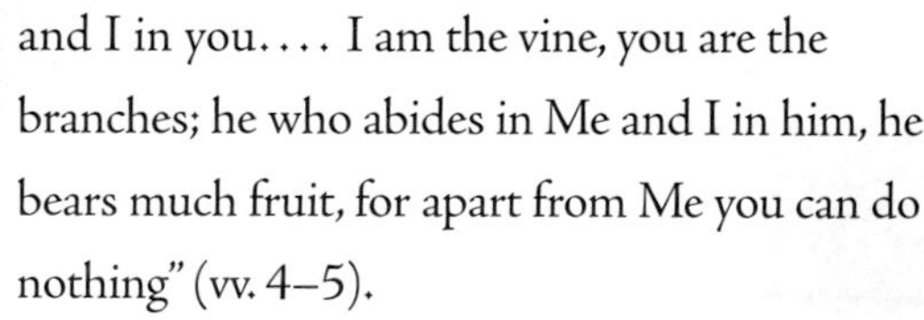

The person who abides in the Lord lives not for himself but for Jesus Christ. I discovered that it was *not* my responsibility to strive for anything. My part was to submit my life to God and allow Him to live His life through me. At my discovery, an enormous weight was lifted and removed from my life. Peace unlike anything I'd ever known filled my life. The energy and strength that ran through the life of Jesus Christ became mine.

In abiding, we discover that God takes our thoughts and conforms them to His will and purpose. He sharpens our talents, purifies our minds, and prepares us for service in His kingdom.

Our treasures—the things we hold dear—become offerings of praise and worship to Him. We begin doing what He has called us to do at the right pace and in the right way. Learning how to plan with His goals in mind is crucial to every area of life. He wants to refocus our spiritual eyesight so we see only Him and not the things that make us feel fearful, insecure, or unsure. We don't have to waste valuable time, and we don't have to work compulsively to do our best. He has the right pace set for us to travel. We can rest because He is in control of all things and because we know that He has a plan and purpose for our existence (Jeremiah 29:11).

IN ABIDING, WE DISCOVER THAT GOD SHARPENS OUR TALENTS, PURIFIES OUR MINDS, AND PREPARES US FOR SERVICE IN HIS KINGDOM.

Your Personal MISSION

Delight yourself also
in the Lord,
And He shall give
you the desires of
your heart.
Commit your way to
the Lord,
Trust also in Him,
And He shall bring it
to pass.

PSALM 37:4–5 NKJV

I OFTEN ENCOURAGE THOSE in my congregation to write a mission statement for their lives, and you should do the same. Ask God to show you how He wants you to live your life. You are never too young or too old to set goals with His mission in mind. Each person who dedicates his or her life to God is given a valuable role to play in His kingdom.

We may not realize the impact of our lives on others. However, God does. He is looking for people who are willing to serve Him. When we say yes to His plans, He will take care of all the details.

Ask Him, "Lord, how do You want me to invest my life?" It may involve something other than your vocation—a job may or may not represent your life purpose. We are called to be Christ's disciples in *every* area of life. Peter, Andrew, and John spent three years with the Savior. During that time, Jesus laid a basic foundation for their lives.

There was an eternal definition to their lives because they walked and talked with the Savior each day. The same can be true for your life. Whether you fully know it or not, God is personally involved in your life. He loves you with an everlasting love, and He wants you to draw near to Him so He can demonstrate His love to you. No matter what has happened in the past, He has plans that stretch far beyond this moment in time.

One of the basics of the Christian life is the act of spending time with Christ. When our lives and hearts are focused on Him, we will discover His purpose and will for our lives.

WHEN YOU COMMIT YOUR WAY TO GOD, HE WILL PLACE YOU IN THE POSITION HE WANTS YOU TO OCCUPY. IT IS A MATTER OF SIMPLE, BASIC TRUST IN GOD.

Often people become entrapped by the question, *What does God want me to do?* This is easy to do, especially when there is a push to know exactly where you are going—what you will declare as your major and what you hope to do after graduation. His Word says, "Trust in the Lord with all your heart and do not lean on your own understanding. In all your ways acknowledge Him, and He will make your paths straight" (Proverbs 3:5–6). When you commit your way to God, He positions you for blessing and for godly success. This may not include success from the world's perspective.

In fact, it usually does not. This does not mean that you will not reach your full potential. Success God's way includes doing what He has given you to do. It is a matter of simple, basic trust in God.

Peace and a sense of satisfaction abide deep within the lives of those who let go of selfish desires so they can experience the reality of God's goodness. Learning to abide instead of striving teaches you to place your trust in Someone who knows much more than you do about life and what is to come. Once you have experienced God's goodness, you will never want to return to a life of striving and self-effort. You will want to know more about your Savior and how your life can more effectively reflect His love and grace to others.

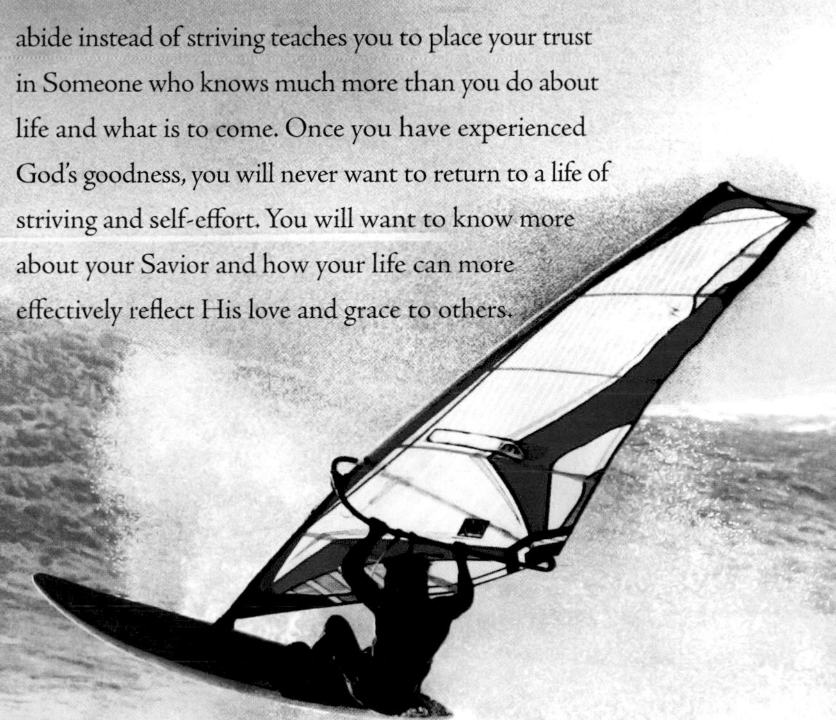

GOD'S *Workmanship*

For we are His workmanship, created in Christ Jesus for good works, which God prepared beforehand so that we would walk in them.

EPHESIANS 2:10

UNDERSTANDING YOUR POSITION IN CHRIST IS THE RUDDER that directs everything you do. Believing the truth about who God says you are—a genuine masterpiece—is essential to your future. You are the creation of God's hands—His imprint is upon you, and He wants you to be a reflection of His glory and character: "We all, with unveiled face, beholding as in a mirror the glory of the Lord, are being transformed into the same image from glory to glory, just as from the Lord, the Spirit" (2 Corinthians 3:18).

He wants you to understand why you were created (and then

re-created through Christ) as well as your purpose in this life. When you understand how beloved you are and the greatness of your purpose, you will be energized to live for God through His power.

God wants us to experience permanent fulfillment. He created us for excellence, and from His perspective, our lives represent infinite possibilities. Trusting Him and understanding His great love for us opens the door to a rich, satisfying life.

WHEN YOU UNDERSTAND HOW BELOVED YOU ARE AND THE GREATNESS OF YOUR PURPOSE, YOU WILL BE ENERGIZED TO LIVE FOR GOD THROUGH HIS POWER.

CHAPTER TWO

GRACE: *Why We Need It*

The direction your life takes is affected by many things, such as the environment in which you live, the decisions you make, and the education you receive. But by far the most powerful influence in a believer's life is the transforming grace of God.

We Are Lost Without CHRIST

But when the kindness of God our Savior and His love for mankind appeared, He saved us, not on the basis of deeds which we have done in righteousness, but according to His mercy, by the washing of regeneration and renewing by the Holy Spirit.

TITUS 3:4–5

OVER THE YEARS, occasionally I have heard someone say, "I guess I'm just going to hell when I die. There is no way for God to love me. I'm beyond His help." No one is ever beyond the grip of God. He loves us, and He created each one of us in love and for His good pleasure. No one in his right mind should speak so carelessly! It is true that each one of us will spend eternity in either heaven or hell, but God wants us to know that He came to die for our sins. He has given us every advantage so that we will accept Him as our Savior and Lord.

Those who have a personal relationship with Jesus Christ know this unfailing truth: our unconditionally loving heavenly Father sent His only begotten Son, Jesus, into this wicked, vile, sinful world to die on a cruel Roman cross. There, He paid the sin-debt of all humanity in order to atone for our sin and reconcile us to God. When you receive Christ by faith as your personal Savior, your eternal destiny is transformed. One moment lost, and the next moment saved. Formerly

headed for hell, now with a home in heaven.

If we do nothing else in our lives, we must reckon with God and accept His free gift of eternal life in Christ. Without His grace, we are utterly without hope. But with His grace, we have an unshakable foundation and the promise of a glorious future.

As a student and someone who has a bright future, this truth is very important. It means once you accept Christ as your Savior, you are no longer alone. You can turn to Him and ask for His help when you are studying for a final, as well as when you are preparing your course schedule for the next term. He is walking with you every step of the way. He knows when you are battling disappointment over lack of funds or grades that ended up not meeting your expectation. He wants you to know that you are not a failure. You are His and He is committed to you and your future.

WHEN YOU RECEIVE CHRIST BY FAITH AS YOUR PERSONAL SAVIOR, YOUR ETERNAL DESTINY IS TRANSFORMED.

Our Great SAVIOR

Jesus . . . because He continues forever, holds His priesthood permanently. Therefore He is able also to save forever those who draw near to God through Him, since He always lives to make intercession for them.

HEBREWS 7:24–25

SOME ASK WHY we celebrate the resurrection. The main reason is Jesus, our Lord and Savior, is alive. No other religious leader who ever lived and died can say this. Only Christ arose from the dead. It is very important for you to understand the resurrection because the same power—His resurrection power—is living in you today through the presence of the Holy Spirit.

We celebrate an empty tomb because the One we love, follow, and serve is no longer there. Now, if the Savior rose from the dead, where is He? Scripture tells us that He is seated at the right hand of God interceding on your behalf.

When you pray, He prays for you, telling the Father your needs, your heartaches, and your deepest desires (Hebrews 7:25). Moreover, Jesus is preparing a place for you and me to be with Him in heaven (John 14:2–3). In the meantime, He is arranging all the events necessary for your future and for His return.

First John 2:1–2 reminds us that the Lord is our Advocate. You see, when the Son of God saved us, He knew we would not live perfect lives—He knew we would sin against Him. So He stands between us and the Father to present our case. This defense is based not merely upon our confession and repentance for the forgiveness of sin, but upon the fact that He laid down His life and paid our sin-debt in full. When Jesus went to the cross, He died a substitutionary, sacrificial death on our behalf. So we can be absolutely confident that our sins are totally forgiven. Salvation has nothing to do with our behavior, but it has everything to do with the grace, love, goodness, and mercy of God, and the blood of Jesus Christ.

His resurrection has given us a very definite purpose for being alive. He has saved us for the purpose of reflecting His life in our work, our ways, our words, and our walk. That is why you and I are the body of Christ. He is looking through our eyes, hearing through our ears, speaking through our voices, and helping through our hands. Having created us for Himself, He desires that you and I walk in holiness and righteousness before Him. We are to be Christ's representatives, pointing people to Him and reflecting His light to a dark world that desperately needs Him.

THE RESURRECTION OF JESUS CHRIST HAS GIVEN US A VERY DEFINITE PURPOSE FOR BEING ALIVE. HE HAS SAVED US FOR THE PURPOSE OF REFLECTING HIS LIFE IN OUR WORK, OUR WAYS, OUR WORDS, AND OUR WALK.

God's Love Frees Us from BONDAGE

It was for freedom that Christ set us free; therefore keep standing firm and do not be subject again to a yoke of slavery.

GALATIANS 5:1

ACCEPTING THE INCREDIBLY expansive love of God is not easy. Many people live their lives convinced that the distance they feel from God must be linked to some sin. They pray incessantly for forgiveness, even trying to find sins that are simply not there. It may be hard to believe, but there are strong Christians who live this way, harboring feelings of shame and self-doubt that have more to do with their fear of intimacy than with reality.

Others know they are saved but have never discovered the true joy and contentment that comes from knowing God in a loving and intimate way. One of the primary reasons the apostle Paul wrote to the believers in Colossae was to express the awesome freedom that is available to us through Jesus Christ. False teachers had entered the fellowship of this New Testament church. They were teaching that while it was right to accept Jesus as the Messiah, one also must live under the regulations of the Mosaic law. Jesus came to set us free from the burden of tradition and regulations. We can obey His law because it has been given to us as a framework for living the abundant life. Nothing brings

greater joy than knowing that you can obey God and receive His blessings in endless number.

However, we cannot attest to God's work of grace while living under the bondage of the law. Completeness is found only in Jesus, not in abiding by prescribed rules or regulations. But we always need to remember that freedom in Christ was a very costly price for God to pay. He gave His Son so that we can live each day in the light of His freedom and hope. Never abuse the gift that He has given you by knowingly entering into sin. When He tells you to steer clear of sin, He does this for a reason. Most of the time, it is to protect and keep you from harm and danger. Sin destroys, while the love of God brings freedom.

MANY PEOPLE KNOW THEY ARE SAVED BUT HAVE NEVER DISCOVERED THE TRUE JOY AND CONTENTMENT OF BEING CHILDREN OF GOD.

The Christian life is an expression of God's grace rather than a checklist of dos and don'ts. It is an overflow of Jesus Christ. That is what Christianity is all about—freedom to enjoy the life God has given us and freedom to share this truth with others.

AN ENCOUNTER *with Grace*

There are many plans in a man's heart, Nevertheless the Lord*'s counsel— that will stand.*

PROVERBS 19:21 NKJV

THE DIRECTION YOUR LIFE TAKES IS AFFECTED BY MANY THINGS, such as the environment in which you live, the decisions you make, and the education you receive. But by far the most powerful influence in a believer's life is the transforming grace of God, which is His kindness toward you regardless of your worthiness and in spite of everything you deserve.

God's ultimate will is for every believer to be conformed to the likeness of His Son. His grace is responsible for your rebirth, and from that point it directs, moves, and influences you to become increasingly Christlike. In that way, you can say with the apostle Paul, "By the grace of God I am what I am" (1 Corinthians 15:10).

The apostle's life, in fact, is a powerful example of God's transforming grace. In Philippians 3, Paul described how he once depended on his good works, nature, and conduct to gain acceptance before God. He did not originally understand there is only one way to be made acceptable in God's sight—by His grace.

However, encountering the living Christ totally changed Paul, and he explained, "Whatever things were gain to me, those things I have [now] counted as loss" (Philippians 3:7). He recognized that all of his human titles and achievements had absolutely no spiritual value. We, too, must realize we will never gain eternity by depending on anything we are or anything we do. It is by grace, and grace alone, that we are saved (Ephesians 2:8–9).

It was the grace of God that shaped Paul's thinking. He learned that everything he once had counted as valuable actually was worthless. What made the difference was the fact that Paul came face-to-face with the Savior on the Damascus Road. When he heard the voice of God speaking to him, he dropped to his knees in adoration and surrender.

IT IS OUT OF HIS GENTLE LOVE—NOT OUT OF CONDEMNATION OR CHASTISEMENT—THAT OUR HEAVENLY FATHER ARRANGES OUR CIRCUMSTANCES AND CHALLENGES.

Life Principles

Is God talking to your heart? Is He asking you to do something you don't like or something you are afraid to do? Remember that it is out of His gentle love—not out of condemnation or chastisement—that the heavenly Father arranges the circumstances and challenges of your life. Whatever He requires of you is always in your best interest and will be part of the process that conforms you to the image of His Son.

for the Graduate

Just like it was with the apostle Paul, an encounter with God's grace will change your course—and it will always lead you in the best possible direction. Therefore, you should always accept His gracious plan because He knows the future. He sees all the potential pitfalls, challenges, and blessings that will come your way. He knows the right way around danger and the very place of safety where you can rest in Him.

CHAPTER THREE

CONNECTING WITH GOD:

The Most Effective Way to Live

If we set our hearts and minds to know God, He will open our spiritual eyes and ears, revealing Himself in wonderful and often unexpected ways. Although the world offers enticing substitutes, nothing can compare to the value of a genuine, growing, passionate relationship with Jesus Christ.

THE TREASURE *of Knowing Christ*

Thus says the Lord, "Let not a wise man boast of his wisdom, and let not the mighty man boast of his might, let not a rich man boast of his riches; but let him who boasts boast of this, that he understands and knows Me."

JEREMIAH 9:23–24

KNOWING JESUS AS OUR LORD radically rearranges our priorities, alters our perspective, and influences our relationships and decision-making processes. Christ becomes the focus and center of our entire lives. In His presence, we gain indescribable peace—a peace so great that we hunger for more.

Prestige, possessions, losses, and heartaches are but "rubbish" when compared with the blessing of knowing Jesus (Philippians 3:8). Discovering His faithfulness, experiencing His help, and embracing His purposes bring meaning and significance to every facet of life.

Paul valued the living, experiential knowledge of Jesus Christ as life's highest goal. He was willing to undergo harsh treatment and imprisonment if the adversity would help him to know his Savior more fully. He could tolerate his afflictions because he viewed them in the light of a broader spiritual goal: experiencing and knowing the sufficiency of Christ in every situation.

Have you come to the point where you can agree with Paul's confession of dependence on Christ? Do you see the suffering you are facing as a means to know

Him in a very personal way? He is close to the brokenhearted. You may be battling temptation, and you can't believe God would continue to love you. He does. He hates sin, but He loves the sinner. And if you will admit your need, He will give you the strength to conquer every temptation, challenge, and sin.

Is knowing Christ your ultimate goal? If it is, then He will show you how to lay your disappointments and failures at the foot of His cross.

God's promises are sure. When we set our hearts and minds to know Him, He opens our eyes and ears to spiritual truth, revealing Himself in wonderful and often unexpected ways. Although the world offers enticing substitutes, nothing can compare to the value of a genuine, growing relationship with Jesus Christ. We read in Colossians 2:3 that "all the treasures of wisdom and knowledge" are hidden in Christ. When our foremost passion is to know God, He assures us He will provide for the rest of our needs (Matthew 6:33).

ALTHOUGH THE WORLD OFFERS ENTICING SUBSTITUTES, NOTHING CAN COMPARE TO THE VALUE OF A GENUINE, GROWING, PASSIONATE RELATIONSHIP WITH JESUS CHRIST.

God Wants to BE KNOWN

The God of our fathers has chosen you that you should know His will, and see the Just One, and hear the voice of His mouth. For you will be His witness to all men of what you have seen and heard.

ACTS 22:14–15 NKJV

THERE IS QUITE A DIFFERENCE between knowing something about God and knowing God in a personal, loving way. Far too many people know about Him but do not really know the person of Jesus Christ. Their relationship with Him may be very superficial. Knowing Jesus Christ involves a progressively deeper understanding through cultivating an intimate relationship with Him.

Too many Christians are content to know Jesus only as their Savior. They are grateful that their sins are forgiven, and that heaven is their destiny. But they are content and unwilling to pursue the real meaning of eternal life: knowing Jesus (John 17:3).

Nothing pleases God more than our full surrender, and He rewards it abundantly. Jesus said, "The one who comes to Me I will certainly not cast out" (John 6:37). It is never God's fault when our relationship with Him wanes. More than anything else, our Father in heaven wants an intimate relationship with His children.

Knowing God involves a cost, and some people are unwilling to pay the price. But for any relationship to grow, we must spend time communicating, listening, and making an effort to understand more about the other person.

Do you really want to know God? The way to do that is by knowing Christ: receive Him as your Savior who paid your sin-debt in full. Then, accept His invitation to spend time in private conversation every day—He wants your undivided attention. And in return, you will receive the incredible opportunity to have a personal, loving relationship with the God of the universe.

You can know His will, His mind, and understand why He works the way He does. He allows disappointment. There will be times that you fail a test—either in the classroom at college or in the classroom of life. When you do, knowing Him makes all the difference. Suddenly, you realize He is on your team and only wants the best for you. Do you know how to trust Him? Do you believe that He has His best for you? It is true. He knows you by name, and He longs to give you His very best—not just for today but for eternity.

FOR ANY RELATIONSHIP TO GROW, WE MUST SPEND TIME COMMUNICATING, LISTENING, AND MAKING AN EFFORT TO UNDERSTAND MORE ABOUT THE OTHER PERSON.

SEEKING THE LORD *with All Your Heart*

"My sheep hear My voice, and I know them, and they follow Me."

JOHN 10:27

TO SPEND TIME WITH THE LORD and hear His voice, you must be still and be quiet. Let's say you're seeking an answer to a pressing need. The most effective way to find the answer is to read and meditate on God's Word. Then pray to Him. Ask Him for His wisdom and help. Then be quiet and listen for His response. Oftentimes, His answer doesn't come when we're praying; it comes when we're not praying. I think sometimes God delays so that we don't get in the habit of sending up "quick fix-it" prayers. By asking Him and then listening for His response, we sometimes "hear" through circumstances or other revelations.

The more time you spend with the Lord, the more familiar His voice becomes. It's like a cloud clearing from your mind. You know without a doubt that God is speaking to you. How does He do this? He speaks to us primarily through His Word. He also will speak through godly, committed believers and through the presence of the Holy Spirit, who abides within us. I can remember in my own life praying and asking God to give me guidance for a situation that I was facing.

Stress was building, and I could not immediately see how He would solve my problems. I believed He would, but it was a matter of walking by faith and trusting Him. Sure enough, as I was praying one day, I sensed Him saying to me: "Trust Me." That was it. These were the two words that drew me nearer to Him and changed my perspective from one of stress to one of power and strength because I knew that His promises do not fail.

He tells us, "Trust in the LORD will all your heart and do not lean on your own understanding. In all your ways acknowledge Him, and He will make your paths straight" (Proverbs 3:5–6). When the bottom to life falls out, you can trust God. He is faithful and true.

As a student, there will be times when you do not know what is best. You may find yourself worrying and wondering which way to go. Don't ever be hesitant to ask Him to speak to you through His Word. He wants you to come to Him. In fact, some of the greatest lessons I have learned have come as a result of going

THE MORE FREQUENTLY YOU SPEND TIME WITH THE LORD, THE MORE FAMILIAR HIS VOICE BECOMES. AND WHEN YOU HEAR HIS ANSWER, YOU CAN FACE THE WORLD.

through times of extreme difficulty. And when you hear His answer, you can face the world. You know with absolute certainty that God has told you what He's going to do. And He always keeps His word.

Throughout all these years, God has never failed me. He has kept every promise that He has ever made to me. Always. There have been times when I wanted to force an answer from Him, but that never works. God has a perfect timetable. He knows exactly when to bring the answer you need. When you ask for something that's not God's best, there should be a check in your spirit—something that says, "Beware. That is not right or God's way." It usually creates a bit of doubt and is an opportunity for you to go to Him in prayer and ask Him to make His will clear.

Over the years, people have said to me, "You mean God cares about this small need or issue in my life?" And I always say, "Absolutely." He cares about everything that involves us. He may not care if you have hot or cold coffee to drink, but He cares about every problem, challenge, or dilemma you encounter. And keep in mind that if your petition is not God's best, He will not give you total peace and assurance.

Spiritual intimacy requires quiet moments when He can speak clearly to your heart and when you can speak honestly to Him.

We need to spend time alone in prayer, meditation, and worship. We come to hear from Him, not just receive from Him. We come to adore Him, praise Him, and delight in Him.

We also must give ourselves to the study of Scripture. The Bible reveals who God is and what He has done. If we really want to know Him, we will set aside time to partake of the living Word, letting His divine counsel saturate our minds. Reading spiritual biographies of godly people can further augment our walk with God as we observe how He has worked in their lives. They have a great deal to tell us about His ways.

I encourage you to lay aside any desire in your life that supersedes your passion to know Christ. Jesus wants all of you, not just a part. You can start today. You can begin to know God on a new, deeper level by admitting your need and asking Him to lead you into the knowledge of Him. When knowing God becomes the passion of your life, you, too, can learn to "count all things to be loss in view of the surpassing value of knowing Christ Jesus" (Philippians 3:8).

God Our FATHER

You have received a spirit of adoption as sons by which we cry out, "Abba! Father!"

ROMANS 8:15

WHEN YOU PRAY, by what name do you address God? While all of the grandiose titles we have given Him are appropriate, we have the awesome privilege of calling God "Father." We can also *know* Him that way. I'll never forget the day this reality came to life in me. I was seated in my office when our administrative assistant walked in with her nine-month-old baby. I stood to admire the infant, and before I could offer a word of praise, she thrust the child into my arms. As I looked down at the tiny baby, I realized she was the same age I was when my father died. Whenever people asked me about him, I simply told them that he died when I was too young to know him. But as I stood holding that baby, I realized that *he* had known *me*. Our relationship with God is the same. He tells us, "Before I formed you in the womb I knew you, and before you were born I consecrated you..." (Jeremiah 1:5).

The possibility of having a personal relationship with God was a revolutionary concept before Christ lived as a human (Matthew 6:9). The Old Testament contains only fifteen references to God as "Father," and those speak primarily of Him as the Father of the Hebrew people. The idea of Him being a personal God to individuals is not evident until the New Testament. Yet that is the reason Jesus Christ came to earth—to die on the cross for our sins and to reveal the heavenly Father so that you and I can know Him intimately.

The privilege of knowing God as Father involves more than acquaintance with Him as a Person. It goes beyond simple familiarity with His matchless grace, love, and kindness, and even surpasses knowing Him in His holiness, righteousness, and justice. How wonderful that we—mere creations—are able to know Him personally as our very own heavenly Parent.

Do you know God as your heavenly Father? If not, realize that He stands ready to adopt you into His family (Romans 8:15; Galatians 3:26). All it takes is a committed desire to know and trust His Son, Jesus Christ, as your personal Savior.

THAT IS THE REASON JESUS CHRIST CAME TO EARTH—TO DIE ON THE CROSS FOR OUR SINS AND TO REVEAL THE HEAVENLY FATHER SO THAT YOU AND I CAN KNOW HIM INTIMATELY.

God Speaks to Us TODAY

Call to Me and I will answer you, and I will tell you great and mighty things, which you do not know.

JEREMIAH 33:3

THE GOD WE SERVE IS NOT A DISTANT, SILENT DEITY. He has been communicating with His creation since the beginning (Genesis 2:16), occasionally by an audible voice, but also in other ways (Exodus 4:4, Hebrews 1:1). Since the first century, He has spoken to us through His Son (Hebrews 1:2), and He continues to speak as we read Scripture, pray, and seek godly counsel from other believers.

You might wonder, *Why would God want to communicate today? What does He have to say to us?* I believe there are several reasons God speaks. The first is that He loves us and desires an intimate bond with His children. As with any growing relationship, conversation has to flow in two directions: we must be willing not only to talk to Him, but also to listen to Him.

A second reason is to give us guidance. God's people today need as much wisdom and counsel as did the saints of the Bible—we still require direction regarding finances, family, career, church, health, and daily life. Divine wisdom is essential if we are to make sound

decisions. This is the reason God sent the Holy Spirit to be our Guide and Teacher (John 16:13, 14:26).

Another reason for His speaking is to bring us comfort and assurance. In Scripture, God spoke to numerous people undergoing hardships and persecution, reminding them of His sovereign control over their situations and fortifying their faith. We are no different from the people in biblical times—just as the children of Israel needed God's confidence to cross the Red Sea, you and I go through turbulent experiences in our lives, and our faith also needs to be strengthened.

A final reason—and, I believe, the primary one—is that God wants us to know Him. Though we can never fully grasp all the facets and wonders of who God is, He wants us to spend our lives discovering more and more about Him. He speaks to you, His child, in order to reveal more of His limitless qualities.

GOD WANTS US TO KNOW HIM. THOUGH WE CAN NEVER FULLY GRASP ALL THE FACETS AND WONDERS OF WHO GOD IS, HE WANTS US TO SPEND OUR LIVES DISCOVERING MORE AND MORE ABOUT HIM.

WHAT A FRIEND *We Have in Jesus*

You will make known to me the path of life; In Your presence is fullness of joy; In Your right hand there are pleasures forever.

PSALM 16:11

I'VE LIVED ALONE FOR THE PAST TWELVE YEARS. If somebody had told me over a decade ago that I could do it, I'd have said, "No way." And yet today I have the most amazing sense of peace, happiness, and joy in my heart because I know I'm never really alone. There was a time when walking into my empty home bothered me, but after a while the Lord reminded me that He is always with me. I think of how much more time I have these days to spend with Him. He turned what, at first, was my complaint into a real comfort. I know now that He is adequate and that He will turn the lonely hours into a fruitful time in my life. In fact, He's already done that.

There is no substitute for personal intimacy with God. Nothing compares with it—it is the key to everything. Most people are looking for an exciting and fulfilling life, and they're looking in all the wrong places: money, prestige, and relationships—mostly relationships. They are looking for something that they can achieve to bring about fulfillment or someone they can meet who will make their small life grow. But there isn't anything we can do or anyone we can meet who will sufficiently fill the void in our hearts. As Thomas Aquinas said, "There is a God-shaped void in all of us." The only thing that can fill the indescribable longing within each human heart is God's presence. The gift of His Son abiding in us is totally adequate for everything we do.

I HAVE THE MOST AMAZING SENSE OF PEACE, HAPPINESS, AND JOY IN MY HEART BECAUSE I KNOW I'M NEVER REALLY ALONE.

In order to experience intimacy with the heavenly Father, you must genuinely regard Him as more important than everything else you pursue in life. It is important to have goals and relationships, but your primary pursuit should be to know God. When I think about all the things I have been through in my life, I consider my relationship with God absolutely paramount. He has always been there to assure me and bring me through life's trials, no matter how hard they have been.

CHAPTER FOUR

TRUSTING THE LORD:

His Purpose Will Move Heaven and Earth

God loves us flawlessly. Every action He performs or permits in our lives is an expression of His love, even though He allows some situations that we think could not possibly be for our good. Although we may not understand His reason for allowing certain hardships, our difficulties in no way indicate He is anything but a good God.

GOD IS *Trustworthy*

Faithful is He who calls you, and He also will bring it to pass.

I THESSALONIANS 5:24

DO YOU TRUST GOD WITH YOUR LIFE? He created you and knows you completely. He understands your weaknesses and your desire to love Him. Even when you feel as though you have failed Him, He is quick to receive you and prove His love to you.

After the Crucifixion, the disciples returned to their former ways of life. Instead of living by faith and doing what God had called them to do, they went right back out on the Sea of Galilee to fish (John 21:3–4)! Have you ever wondered how God views our lack of faith? It is certain that He will never condemn us (Romans 8:1). Christ's presence on the shore of Galilee was enough to let Peter and the others know that it was time to stop being distracted by the voices of the world. Before the Crucifixion, He had told the disciples that He would return to them, and He fulfilled His promise. God

has kept every promise He has ever made. This is why we can trust Him with every aspect of our lives.

Although Peter denied knowing Christ, Jesus did not deny knowing him. We may falter and fail, but God does not want us to focus on our shortcomings. Instead, He wants us to set our focus on Him. God evaluates our lives not according to our ability to remain faithful, but according to *His* faithfulness and the work that was accomplished at Calvary. While He does not want us to yield to temptation, He knows there will be times when we fall. But always we remain the beneficiaries of His endless grace and eternal love. After the resurrection, one of the first things Jesus did was to go to Peter and reassure him of His eternal love. God's plan for Peter's life had not changed. Therefore, Jesus encouraged His disciple not to give up. A person who lives by faith will recognize the fact that God never gives up on him.

GOD HAS KEPT EVERY PROMISE HE HAS EVER MADE. THIS IS WHY WE CAN TRUST HIM WITH EVERY ASPECT OF OUR LIVES.

Our Lives Are in HIS HANDS

The counsel of the
LORD stands forever,
The plans of His
heart from generation
to generation. . . .
Our heart rejoices
in Him,
Because we trust in
His holy name.

PSALM 33:11, 21

OUR LIVES BELONG TO OUR SOVEREIGN, all-knowing, loving God, and nothing can touch us except what He allows. Sometimes that includes hardship and suffering, which leaves us wondering, *How can this possibly be good?* And yet many people who have gone through tremendous trials later look back and say, "I hated the difficulty while I was going through it and wondered if God had deserted me. But now, on this side of it, I can see why He allowed it." Not everyone fully understands the spiritual insight. Yet it happens frequently enough that we can take comfort, realizing that God has His purposes and, with perfect timing, will bring blessing from our trials (Romans 8:28).

When you face struggles, remind yourself that God has your best interest in mind. He wants you to trust Him as your personal Savior and to surrender your life to Him. There is no reason to doubt Him because He is perfect in His love, infinite in His wisdom, and sovereign in His control of the entire universe. Why should believers ever fret when, even in the deepest, darkest valleys, there can be abiding joy and confidence? No matter what befalls you, our all-loving, all-wise, all-powerful heavenly Father has you in the cradle of His hand.

HE IS PERFECT IN HIS LOVE, INFINITE IN HIS WISDOM, AND SOVEREIGN IN HIS CONTROL OF THE ENTIRE UNIVERSE.

WALKING *in Christ*

If we live by the Spirit, let us also walk by the Spirit.

GALATIANS 5:25

SCRIPTURE FREQUENTLY USES THE EXAMPLE of walking as a description of believers' behavior. For example, we are told to walk as children of light, walk in the truth, walk according to the Spirit, and walk in love. Colossians 2:6 uses this expression to give us an important command: "As you have received Christ Jesus as Lord, so walk in Him." The question we must ask is, "What does it mean to walk in Christ?"

Here the word *in* does not have a literal usage, like "the hammer is *in* the toolbox." Rather, it refers to a vital relationship—a union between the believer and the Lord. What God desires is not simply to forgive sins, but to develop a close, ever-deepening, personal relationship with each of His children. He wants us to realize that the Son of God is the source of everything—Jesus Christ is to the believer what blood is to the body: indispensable to life.

Therefore, "walking in Christ" refers to a dynamic relationship with the Lord. Just as it is impossible to walk while standing still, believers are either moving

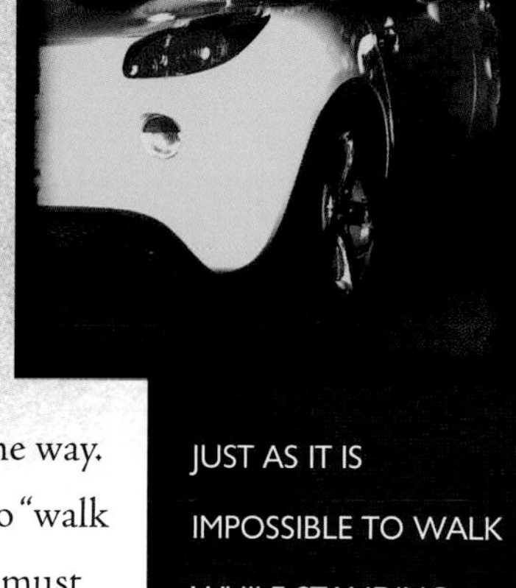

forward in their Christian life or falling backward. The key for making progress is found in that same Colossians verse: "As you have received Christ Jesus the Lord, so walk in Him." How did you and I receive Christ? By faith. In order to be born again, we trusted the testimony of God's Word. The Christian life is to be "walked"—or lived out—in the same way.

Followers of Jesus Christ are commanded to "walk by faith, not by sight" (2 Corinthians 5:7). We must take the first step by faith, and then another step by trusting that our omniscient, loving God has our best interest in mind. Walking in faith means having a personal relationship with Jesus Christ that results in trusting Him for every circumstance and believing He will do what is right and what benefits us every time, without exception.

JUST AS IT IS IMPOSSIBLE TO WALK WHILE STANDING STILL, BELIEVERS ARE EITHER MOVING FORWARD IN THEIR CHRISTIAN LIFE OR FALLING BACKWARD.

THE WAY *of Faith*

And we know that God causes all things to work together for good to those who love God, to those who are called according to His purpose.

ROMANS 8:28

WHAT DO YOU DO WHEN FACING A CHALLENGE that seems insurmountable? Proverbs 3:5–6 instructs you to "trust in the LORD with all your heart and do not lean on your own understanding. In all your ways acknowledge Him, and He will make your paths straight."

God has a purpose for every situation we encounter. There are no coincidences with Him. He is the Architect behind every blessing that comes our way. In times of trial and sorrow, He is working in ways unknown to us to bring goodness and hope out of each difficulty.

When God commanded him to sacrifice his only son on the altar, Abraham did not cower in fear or lay awake at night wondering how the Lord would provide for him. He trusted God, and in doing so, he was able to have fellowship with Him. Scripture tells us that Abraham believed God, and his belief was "reckoned" to him as "righteousness" (Genesis 15:6).

There are two things that are essential to living a faith-motivated life. First, we must believe that God exists. Second, we must believe that He will do what He has promised to do. Hebrews 11:6 tells us that "without faith it is impossible to please [God], for he who comes to God must believe that He is and that He is a rewarder of those who seek Him." Faith is not a goal that we must work to achieve. It comes as the overflow of a personal relationship with God. It is as natural as taking a breath of air. Faith is the breath and life of our relationship with God and His Son.

GOD HAS A PURPOSE FOR EVERY SITUATION WE ENCOUNTER. THERE ARE NO COINCIDENCES WITH HIM.

Making Our Faith STRONG

On God my salvation and my glory rest;
The rock of my strength, my refuge is in God.
Trust in Him at all times, O people;
Pour out your heart before Him;
God is a refuge for us.

PSALM 62:7–8

GOD HAS A PLAN TO DEVELOP OUR FAITH. He takes our limited trust and grows it into a strong and mighty faith—one that has the ability to conquer deadly foes. This is often why He allows us to face adversity and challenges of all kinds, good and bad. In times of extreme pressure, God stretches our faith and deepens our dependence on Him. Without strong, abiding trust, we will quickly yield to temptation and fear, especially when the trial or difficulty is intense or prolonged.

God developed David's trust until it became unshakable, and He wants to do this in our lives as well. Whether it relates to the beginning of a new chapter or the ending of an old one, God wants to teach us to trust Him at every turn in life.

One of Satan's primary attacks in the life of a believer is discouragement. Even Jesus warned us not to be concerned about the one who could kill our bodies but, instead, to be aware of the one who could kill our souls. Once we have accepted Christ as our Savior, the enemy assumes a different role. He goes to work on our emotions by trying to persuade us to believe that God doesn't really love us and that we are not worthy of His love and affection. He seeks ways to cause us to feel defeated and discouraged with the goal that if he can make us give up, then we will abandon our commitment and love for God.

However, Satan cannot defeat the love of God. God's love for us is paramount and eternal. He loves us not because of what we do, but because of what His Son did for us on Calvary's cross. There is nothing we can do to become worthy of God's unconditional love. It is simply there for the taking, whenever we are ready to accept it and ask Him to show us how to appropriate it in our lives.

GOD WANTS TO TEACH US TO TRUST HIM AT EVERY TURN IN LIFE.

The "Goliath" in your life may come in the form of financial troubles, the death of a loved one, news of a serious illness, a broken relationship, or the betrayal of a friend. God does not want us to sink into feelings of doubt and worry. He is our ever-present Help, our Rock, our Fortress, our Deliverer, our Refuge, our Strength, and our infinite Stronghold (Psalm 18).

CHAPTER FIVE

OBEDIENCE: *It Always Means Blessing*

God can revolutionize our lives. For some people, this could mean a change of career, a new location, or a different relationship. Are you willing to do what God says, when and how He says to do it? Are you willing to leave all the consequences to Him? Without a right relationship with Christ, you will never have real contentment, peace, or assurance. Nothing else in this world can ever truly satisfy.

OBEDIENCE *Brings Blessings*

The Lord leads with unfailing love and faithfulness all who keep his covenant and obey his demands.

PSALM 25:10 NLT

ONE OF THE MOST BASIC yet important principles a Christian can ever learn is that of obedience. When we obey God, we will experience His blessing; when we don't, we will miss out on that blessing.

The more familiar we become with God's Word, the more we will begin to understand the importance of obedience. God's laws are not designed to deprive us of pleasure or prosperity. Rather, they are intended to protect us from hurting ourselves and others and to guide us toward the fulfillment in life that He wants us to enjoy.

When we are faced with daily pressures, we may be tempted to compromise Scripture's teaching in favor of self-reliance or worldly solutions. Every person has God-given desires and appetites, which can be satisfied as He intended or in selfish and harmful ways. Throughout our lives, we will encounter opposition to biblical living. Obedience to God involves a commitment to Him, regardless of the consequences.

Obeying God often involves choices that we fear could result in rejection, loss, or hardship. Sometimes the decision to follow Christ brings about unwanted confrontation. Obedience always requires courage. However difficult our circumstances may be, we can respond to them with confidence in the One who empowers us to do His will. Has God ever made a mistake, been too late, or proven inadequate? No! Our heavenly Father is all-powerful and consistently faithful.

The laws of Scripture are profound yet simple: the Bible teaches that we will reap what we sow, and oftentimes, more than we sow. When we obey God, we always get His best. When we don't, life will turn out to be much less than it could be and much harder than it needs to be. We do not always do what we should, and there is grace in those situations; but for Christians, making a commitment to obey God is essential to our faith. Obedience and faith are inseparable. We demonstrate our trust in God by complying with His will. When we do so, we will reap the rewards He has designed for us—and we will hit our target every time.

WHEN WE OBEY GOD, WE ALWAYS GET HIS BEST. WHEN WE DON'T, LIFE WILL TURN OUT TO BE MUCH LESS THAN IT COULD BE AND MUCH HARDER THAN IT NEEDS TO BE.

THE KEY
to God's Heart

Then Jesus said to His disciples, "If anyone wishes to come after Me, he must deny himself, and take up his cross and follow Me. For whoever wishes to save his life will lose it; but whoever loses his life for My sake will find it."

MATTHEW 16:24–25

I STILL REMEMBER THE KEY that unlocked the door to our house. I was in the first grade, and I would hide it under a rock after I left each morning so no one but my mother and I knew where it was. When I came home in the afternoon, I wondered if the key would still be there. A wonderful sense of relief flooded over me when I spotted the key. The key was important to me because it was the key to our home. It unlocked the place where we lived—where my needs were met and where I felt my mother's love and care.

More than likely, you have a set of keys—keys to your house, car, a dorm room door, or some other important entry way. But do you have the key to someone's heart? When you have the key to someone's heart, you know how to reach what is inside. You know how to move that person toward you, and you understand how he or she feels.

The key to God's heart is obedience, but too many people fail to realize this. We're taught to be independent and self-reliant, and the idea of obedience doesn't always go over well with everyone. God does not

OBEDIENCE
Can Turn Everything Around

For thus the Lord GOD, the Holy One of Israel, has said, "In repentance and rest you will be saved, In quietness and trust is your strength."

ISAIAH 30:15

GOD'S SIMPLE REQUESTS are often stepping-stones to life's greatest blessings. Simon Peter gives us a good illustration of what happens when we say yes to God. In Luke 5:1–11, people were pressing in around Jesus while He was preaching. The Lord wanted to use Peter's boat as a floating platform from which to address the throng on shore, so He asked the future apostle to push the vessel out a little way (v. 3). This was not a particularly remarkable request, but Peter's obedience was. He was a seasoned fisherman and knew the waters of the Sea of Galilee in a way that few did. Yet it was his willingness to do what the Savior asked that paved the way for multiple blessings on that day. From his example, we learn just how important it is to obey the Lord, no matter what His request may be.

Immediately, the people were blessed by Peter's obedience because they could hear Jesus' words as He taught. Then, when the lesson was completed, the Lord said to Peter, "Put out into the deep water and let down your nets for a catch" (v. 4). Here was another opportunity for Peter to obey or say no. He had worked the entire night with the hopes of catching a large amount of fish. But he had returned empty-handed and exhausted. Now, Jesus was telling him to head back out onto the Sea of Galilee at a time of day when no one would dare drop his nets. The idea to go fishing probably seemed preposterous! But notice what Peter did and how he responded to the Savior. He obeyed Him, and as a result of his obedience, two overflowing boatloads of fish were pulled to shore (v. 7). Saying yes resulted in a miracle that absolutely transformed Peter's life and the lives of those with him.

Perhaps Peter believed Jesus' instructions would amount to no more than just a waste of time. But when he complied with that simple request, he was gripped with amazement at what the Lord did. Like Peter, we must recognize that obeying God is always the wise course of action. Jesus turned an empty boat into a full one. He can also take our emptiness—whether it is related to finance, relationship, or career—and change it into something splendid and thriving.

WE MUST RECOGNIZE THAT OBEYING GOD IS ALWAYS THE WISE COURSE OF ACTION. JESUS TURNED AN EMPTY BOAT INTO A FULL ONE. HE CAN ALSO TAKE OUR EMPTINESS AND CHANGE IT INTO SOMETHING SPLENDID AND THRIVING.

Obedience—ALWAYS

We are destroying speculations and every lofty thing raised up against the knowledge of God, and we are taking every thought captive to the obedience of Christ.

2 CORINTHIANS 10:5

OBEDIENCE CAN BE A CHALLENGE, especially if we think we know more about our lives and circumstances than God does. However, the inescapable truth is this: obedience is essential to pleasing Him—not just in times of deep, serious temptation, but in moments of simpler testing as well.

Can you remember the last time you were tempted to do the opposite of what you knew God desired you to do? Deep inside, you probably understood what was right, but a struggle ensued in your mind. The question arose: *Should I obey God and please Him or disobey Him and hope that He won't notice?* In truth, nothing good can come from disobeying God, and nothing bad can come from obeying Him. When we decide to obey God, we choose the way of wisdom, which is the way to blessing.

Disobedience sends a message to the Lord declaring that we believe we know better than He does. All sin is pure rebellion against God. However, self-assurance evaporates when it comes face-to-face with the sovereignty of almighty God. When the prophet Isaiah stood in His presence, he cried out, "Woe is me . . . I am a man of unclean lips, and I live among a people of unclean lips" (Isaiah 6:5).

God was looking for someone who would take His Word to the people. And Isaiah was His man. He had seen God's glory, and obedience was his only choice. Can you remember the last time you had a choice to obey God or ignore His commands? Imagine how different things would have turned out if Isaiah had followed a selfish route rather than God's directive.

GOD COMMANDS OUR OBEDIENCE NOT BECAUSE HE IS A STRICT TASKMASTER, BUT BECAUSE HE KNOWS THE EFFECT DISOBEDIENCE AND SIN WILL HAVE ON OUR LIVES.

God's concern for us springs from His deep love and devotion. He requires our obedience because He knows the devastating effect disobedience and sin will have on our lives. There are some consequences to sin that time cannot erase. God forgives and is willing to restore, but some of the wrongs we do have lasting results. Disobedience always leads to disappointment, sorrow, and brokenness. But obedience leads to joy, peace, fulfillment, and security. When you obey God, you will never have an occasion to doubt His goodness toward you.

THE BLESSING *of the Holy Spirit*

Work out your salvation with fear and trembling; for it is God who is at work in you, both to will and to work for His good pleasure.

PHILIPPIANS 2:12–13

MANY PEOPLE THINK THEY ARE DEMONSTRATING OBEDIENCE TO GOD by helping others occasionally, avoiding temptation, and attending church. But there is much more to obedience. True obedience to God means doing *what* He says, *when* He says, *how* He says, *as long as* He says, *until* what He asks us to do is accomplished.

Unfortunately, this concept often is rejected in today's culture. We have rationalized disobedience to the point of missing God's best. Do you ever catch yourself wondering why God doesn't answer your prayers? The answer could lie in your level of obedience to Him. If you have accepted Jesus Christ as your Savior and yet are still experiencing great spiritual frustration, there may be an area of disobedience in your life that you have not addressed.

Perhaps God has asked something of you and, in response, you have ignored His words or done only part of what He requires.

Is there one particular area of your life in which you struggle to be obedient to God's Word? As you read Scripture, does He continually bring a particular sin to your attention? If the Lord is bringing something to your mind right now, it could be that you have been living in the same situation for years because at some point, you chose to do things *your* way instead of *God's* way.

Understanding this key distinction between our way and God's way can make a tremendous difference in every believer's life. To avoid disobedience, you must bring your thoughts, actions, words, and goals in line with God's perfect will (2 Corinthians 10:5). More importantly, when He gives you words of direction, wisdom, or warning, you must heed them completely.

TO AVOID DISOBEDIENCE, YOU MUST BRING YOUR THOUGHTS, ACTIONS, WORDS, AND GOALS IN LINE WITH GOD'S PERFECT WILL.

There is good news: even though we cannot be as perfect and blameless as Christ until we are with Him in heaven, the Holy Spirit enables us to obey Him today. In doing so, we *take on* the Spirit of Christ. We become like Him in the sense that we want to live holy lives and reflect His principles and love to others. No amount of human effort can achieve what God gives through His grace. If it were not possible to live obedient lives, He would have told us. No matter what He requires of us—whether it be painful or joyful, profitable or costly—God Himself will help us to obey and reach our goals.

When you receive Jesus Christ as your Savior, your first act of obedience should be to pray, "Father, forgive me of my sins. I've sinned against You. I've been living in rebellion. I'm asking You to forgive me of my sins, not because I'm so good, but because I believe Jesus paid my sin-debt in full." The moment you do this, the Holy Spirit comes into your heart, and God saves you.

He also enables you to walk obediently before Him, in His strength and in His power.

My prayer for you—my petition on your behalf—is that you will be obedient to God. That way, you can become the person He wants you to be, do the work He desires of you, bear the fruit He enables you to bear, and receive the blessings He has prepared for you.

WHATEVER HE REQUIRES OF US—WHETHER IT BE PAINFUL OR JOYFUL, PROFITABLE OR COSTLY—GOD HIMSELF WILL HELP US TO OBEY.

CHAPTER SIX

GOD'S WILL: *It's Worth the Wait*

God has a plan for your life. That plan is clearly directed from the outset. That is, God does not leave you to guess. God works this way because all of His plans are connected, and He knows that what you do will affect other people as well as yourself, both now and in the future. It is essential that you listen to Him and wait.

WAITING *on the Lord*

Wait for the Lord;
Be strong and let
your heart take
courage;
Yes, wait for
the Lord.

PSALM 27:14

WHEN GOD TELLS US TO WAIT ON HIS WILL, He always has a very clear reason, and that reason is without exception to our benefit. Waiting is essential in living the Christian life, walking in obedience to God, and receiving the best of God's blessings.

Being patient is surely difficult, but failing to wait upon the Lord can bring about disastrous consequences. First, when we do not wait, we get out of God's will. Second, we delay God's planned blessing for us. Because we move ahead of His steps, we get out of cycle and miss God's blessings in *His* time. Third, we bring pain and suffering upon others and ourselves. Throughout Scripture, you can see the resulting pain that people endure from getting out of God's will and doing things their own way. Fourth, we are prone to make snap judgments that quite often turn out to cost us dearly in terms of finances, emotional energy, and relationships.

Many people are not willing to wait on God for His timing, particularly when it involves the possibility of letting go of something they desire desperately. But when we take our eyes off God and try to manipulate our situation to conform to our will, we usually make a colossal mess of things. Whenever we reach for something that is not of God, it turns to ashes. He will never prosper what we manipulate. No matter how hard we try, it just doesn't work. Either we can repent, back off, and wait for the Lord—in which case, more than likely, He'll give us what we ask for—or we can step out ahead of Him and lose it.

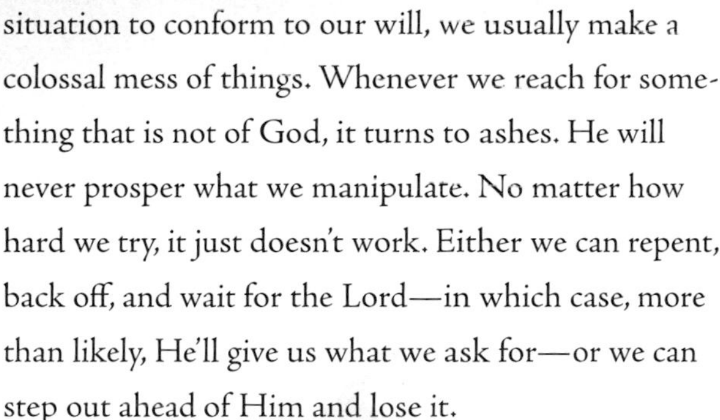

WHEN WE TAKE OUR EYES OFF GOD AND TRY TO MANIPULATE OUR SITUATION TO CONFORM TO OUR WILL, WE USUALLY MAKE A COLOSSAL MESS OF THINGS.

Something may be the will of God, but if you step out ahead of His timing, you can ruin His blessing for your life. We live much happier lives when we learn to obey with grace and trust.

STOP *and Listen*

Yet those who wait
for the Lord
Will gain new
strength;
They will mount
up with wings
like eagles,
They will run and
not get tired,
They will walk and
not become weary.

ISAIAH 40:31

WAITING ON THE LORD DOES NOT MEAN BEING STAGNANT. God is moving and active. He has a definite plan for your life, but He may be calling you to wait awhile, for what purpose I do not know. I pray that you can discover that for yourself, in His time.

One of the primary reasons believers step out of God's will—and out of fellowship with the Lord—is that they begin to go forward with their own plans apart from His wisdom or guidance. They become eager and impatient. Without waiting for clear direction, they move ahead and make decisions without taking time to pray and seek His best. It is important for you to realize what it means to truly wait upon the Lord.

Waiting on the Lord does not require you to be idle. Instead, it simply means pausing until you receive further instructions. You should think of waiting as a determined stillness, during which time you decide not to act until the Lord gives clear direction.

Yes, waiting is hard. It is difficult to stand still when everything in you wants to move. However, wise men and women wait upon the Lord until they have heard from Him. Then, when they finally move, it is with boldness, confidence, courage, strength, and absolute assurance that God will keep His word.

YOU SHOULD THINK OF WAITING AS A DETERMINED STILLNESS, DURING WHICH TIME YOU DECIDE NOT TO ACT UNTIL THE LORD GIVES CLEAR DIRECTION.

STEADFAST *Trust*

Some trust
in chariots, and
some in horses;
But we will
remember the name
of the Lord
our God.

PSALM 20:7 NKJV

THE ONLY WAY TO WAIT PATIENTLY FOR A WORD FROM GOD involves learning how to rest in Him. If you want to hear what He has to say, you must come to the point where you are no longer rushing or running around in your mind. Clearly, you cannot separate waiting upon the Lord and trusting in Him—these two things go hand in hand.

Patient waiting does not involve looking around to see what others are doing. How often have you been sure of what the Lord has said to do, but then you changed your course of action because of what you saw others doing around you? Or how often have you been sure of what the Lord has said, but you felt tempted to doubt Him because of the negative voices you heard? Most people know what it feels like to be headed in one direction only to have a set of questions arise in their minds. *Is this the right choice? How do I know that this is Your best, Lord? What if I make a mistake?* God wants to clear up all the clutter. He has a simple, straightforward path, but you must still your heart so you can discern it.

Waiting demands patience, and it certainly requires trust. As you wait upon the Lord, you will have to stand strong against the pressure of other people who want to goad you into making a decision that fits their schedules and timing. Maybe you are in a relationship or a job and don't feel ready to move ahead. If God has not given you the green light, moving forward at the insistence of others is the worst thing you can do.

When it comes to your personal, private walk with God, the bottom line is this: Are you going to listen to God and do what He says? Are you going to wait upon Him when your peers become impatient and everything around you is pushing you to move?

You can take heart in knowing that God will strengthen you through your waiting. If you trust in Him, then He will help you shoulder the weight of your burdens.

THIS IS THE BOTTOM LINE: ARE YOU GOING TO LISTEN TO GOD AND DO WHAT HE SAYS? ARE YOU GOING TO WAIT UPON HIM WHEN EVERYTHING AROUND YOU IS PUSHING YOU TO MOVE?

When God Seems FAR AWAY

Therefore we do not lose heart, but though our outer man is decaying, yet our inner man is being renewed day by day. For momentary, light affliction is producing for us an eternal weight of glory far beyond all comparison, while we look not at the things which are seen, but at the things which are not seen...

2 CORINTHIANS 4:16–18

THERE ARE TIMES IN EVERY CHRISTIAN'S LIFE WHEN GOD seems distant and uninterested in our circumstances. We pray and diligently seek His will, but our need, at least from our perspective, remains unmet. We wait and wait but do not hear from the Lord. Does God truly have an answer? Does He *really* care when we hurt and struggle against the pressures of life? How should we handle times of spiritual silence when we feel as though He is standing at a distance and is not going to answer our prayers according to our desires and our timeline?

Take a few moments to read the story of Mary, Martha, and Lazarus in John 11. Each of these people had definite needs. Lazarus needed a healing touch from God. He was deathly ill (v. 1), and Jesus had the power to heal him. Mary and Martha had tremendous needs as well. How would they survive without Lazarus? He was the head of their household, and because neither one was married, Lazarus took care of them. Jesus knew that.

In fact, the Lord was their close friend and a frequent guest in their home. Once Mary and Martha realized the sickness of their brother could lead to death, it only seemed right to send for Jesus. More than likely, they knew He cared for them and for Lazarus.

The issue that confronts us in a situation like this one is God's will versus our will. We are taught to pray and to ask God to meet our needs. But there is something deep within this process that the Father wants us to learn. We begin to understand just how committed He is to meeting our needs when we learn to accept His will as being the one true and perfect will. We also must acknowledge that His timing is perfect, just as His strength is sufficient and His love is eternal. Sometimes when we have to wait for God's provision or answer, it seems as if He is completely uninterested in our situation.

WE BEGIN TO UNDERSTAND JUST HOW COMMITTED HE IS TO MEETING OUR NEEDS WHEN WE LEARN TO ACCEPT HIS WILL AS BEING PERFECT.

Life Principles

As their brother lay dying, Mary and Martha did not understand just how deeply involved God was in their lives. At times, each one of us has failed to understand this. Jesus was determined to demonstrate His intimate care for these women and for His friend Lazarus. But first, Mary and Martha would have to wait. And their prayers, though in harmony with God's will, would appear to go unanswered.

Somewhere along the line, Mary and Martha had to deal with the sovereignty of God. They had to come to a point where they accepted God's will over their own. Each one of us will face this decision at some time.

We may wonder why, on the surface, it appears that God has not met our needs. Yet deep inside we should understand that God never leaves us hopeless. He has a plan and a design for our lives that are well fitted for every trial, every sorrow, every heartache, and every problem we face.

Never give up! Trust God to the end, and you *will* see His goodness become a reality in your life.

GOD NEVER LEAVES US HOPELESS. HE HAS A PLAN AND A DESIGN FOR OUR LIVES THAT ARE WELL FITTED FOR EVERY TRIAL, EVERY SORROW, EVERY HEARTACHE, AND EVERY PROBLEM WE FACE.

DETERMINING
God's Will—In Everything

We have not ceased to pray for you and to ask that you may be filled with the knowledge of His will in all spiritual wisdom and understanding.

COLOSSIANS 1:9

GOD DOES NOT WITHHOLD any information that we need regarding His will. But He may not tell us everything. For example, He does not reveal what will happen over the next ten years. Since He wants us to live in trusting dependence upon Him each and every day, He gives us enough light to walk by each day. Remember, His Word is a lamp to our feet, not a floodlight to illuminate the highway clear through to our destination (Psalm 119:105). He desires that you and I know and obey His will for us day by day.

As a pastor, I often hear this common question: "How can I know the will of God?" People ask this not only when they're trying to determine the overall direction their lives should take, but also regarding the smaller, daily decisions. Many are confused about whether it is possible to know the Father's will or if He even has a specific will for their lives.

Be assured: you *can* know God's will, and you can know it for *sure*. You do not have to fret because you

can know with complete certainty God's will for every circumstance of your life. Although He may not disclose every detail about each situation, His Word provides specific steps you can take each day in order to learn and fulfill His will for your life.

When making important decisions, consider the following questions:

- *Is it consistent with the Word of God?* God's Word is full of life principles. A single passage can offer wisdom that applies to so many circumstances.
- *Is this a wise decision?* Ask yourself what the future consequences of choosing one way over another are.
- *Can I honestly ask God to enable me to achieve this?* Remember, anything you acquire outside of God's will sooner or later turns to ashes.

IF YOU ARE IN THE PROCESS OF MAKING A DIFFICULT DECISION AND ARE CONCERNED ABOUT THE CONSEQUENCES, REMEMBER YOU HAVE ENTRUSTED YOUR LIFE TO A LOVING, HEAVENLY FATHER WHO PLANS ONLY THE BEST.

Life Principles

- *Do I have genuine peace about this?* Bring your concern before the Lord. If there isn't a ripple in your heart, your conscience and emotions are saying yes, and you understand God to be saying yes, then you have perfect peace.
- *Does this fit who I am as a follower of Jesus?* All of our actions should be consistent with the fact that we belong to Christ and reflect Him to the world.
- *Does this fit God's overall plan for my life?* If the Lord left all choices up to us, then we would be free to make every decision without considering His will

on the matter. But He has a specific plan for each of His children, and it always is for our best.

- *Will this decision honor God?* Our actions and attitudes should be in keeping with whom we know God to be rather than a statement that we are "doing our own thing."

If you are in the process of making a difficult decision and are concerned about the consequences, remember you have entrusted your life to a loving, heavenly Father who plans only the best, promises only the best, and provides only the best. You simply cannot lose when you obey Him.

Keep Hope ALIVE

This I recall
to my mind,
Therefore
I have hope.
The Lord's loving-
kindnesses indeed
never cease,
For His compassions
never fail.
They are new every
morning;
Great is Your
faithfulness.

LAMENTATIONS 3:21–23

MANY TIMES OUR SPIRITUAL INSIGHT IS LIMITED, but God sees all. He knows exactly what is transpiring on every spiritual level, along with all that we are facing. He has a plan, and if we are wise, we will wait for Him to reveal it to us.

Positive confession is a powerful force in the life of a believer. This does not mean talking boastfully or claiming God's deliverance apart from His expressed will for your life. Thanking God for His faithfulness and provision is an indication of your submission to His will, regardless of your hopes or expectations. Seasons of life may not turn out the way you thought. You may struggle. Mary and Martha watched as their brother died. However, because we serve a risen Lord and Savior, we know that no matter what we face in this life, God will ultimately deliver us from all evil. He will bless us as we seek to know Him intimately. He will guard, protect, and lead us into a place of great blessing and hope.

Have you trusted the Savior with your unmet needs, or are you still focused on satisfying your hopes and desires as quickly as possible? Only God can completely meet your needs. Trust Him—give Him your burden to carry and you will witness a tremendous miracle.

And if you have to be patient, the very act of waiting will strengthen your hope and breathe new life into your being.

THANKING GOD FOR HIS FAITHFULNESS AND PROVISION IS AN INDICATION OF YOUR SUBMISSION TO HIS WILL, REGARDLESS OF YOUR HOPES OR EXPECTATIONS.

CHAPTER SEVEN

ADVERSITY: *He Refines Us by Fire*

Whatever form our trials may take—whether sickness, financial problems, animosity, rejection, bitterness, or anger—we tend to consider them setbacks. God, however, has a different perspective. He views adversity as a way not to hinder the saints, but to advance their spiritual growth.

God is in CONTROL

He will . . . refine them like gold and silver, so that they may present to the L*ORD offerings in righteousness.*

MALACHI 3:3

CLOTH CAN DUST OFF A PIECE OF GOLD, but the metal must be refined to remove embedded impurities. That is, it must be melted by fire so that any tarnish or pollution can rise and be skimmed from the surface.

The Christian life is frequently compared to this process. When we face struggles, God is refining us like precious metal, digging deep into our lives to eliminate all the dirt and pollution. He does this not to hurt us, but to help us grow into beautiful reflections of the life of His Son.

Too often we hear people exclaim, "This world is out of control!" Those with little or no belief in an almighty God of the universe find themselves without any source of strength or encouragement when their world begins to collapse. Family heartache, financial problems, or national tragedies—these are all things that we have witnessed firsthand. In the face of such turmoil, how can we be sure God is in control?

If I had to choose a single book in Scripture that powerfully reveals God's complete control on page after page from beginning to end, it would be Genesis. In this first book of the Bible, we get to see God working through many different circumstances and obstacles. We see Him as the supreme Lord of creation by creating absolutely everything out of absolutely nothing. We see Him providing a way for you and me to conquer sin and death and achieve victory, in spite of the invasion of sin into the world. We see Him destroying every single person on earth with a great flood, but saving one family to repopulate the earth.

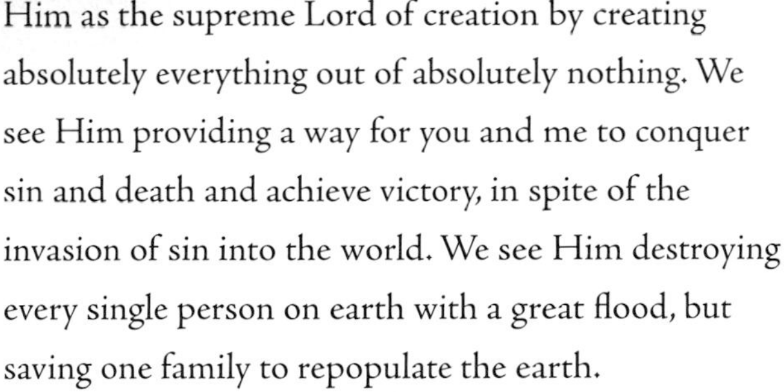

Again and again throughout Genesis, we see this pattern: God plans to do something, and despite human unfaithfulness, His perfect will is accomplished. This is the case throughout all of Scripture, and it is still true today. God is in control despite our pain, questions, turmoil, and selfishness.

GOD IS REFINING US LIKE PRECIOUS METAL, DIGGING DEEP INTO OUR LIVES TO ELIMINATE ALL THE DIRT AND POLLUTION. HE DOES THIS NOT TO HURT US, BUT TO HELP US GROW INTO BEAUTIFUL REFLECTIONS OF HIM.

Take Comfort in God's SOVEREIGNTY

The LORD *of hosts has sworn saying, "Surely, just as I have intended so it has happened, and just as I have planned so it will stand."*

ISAIAH 14:24

WHEN BAD THINGS HAPPEN, some people either deny God's existence or excuse Him from taking responsibility. Why do they do this? For one thing it is clear that many do not understand the Word of God, which clearly teaches God's complete control over creation.

Let me ask you a question: If God is not in control, who is? If no one or nothing is in control, doesn't everything happen as a result of chance or luck? Even Christians throw around the ideas of *luck* and *good fortune*. When I hear this, I immediately know they do not fully understand God's Word. Scripture is clear: there are no coincidences with God. He knows what is going to happen even before it takes place. And there is no such thing as sheer luck. He is sovereign and He is over all things. Everything is subject to Him and His will.

If we replace His sovereignty with sheer luck, we are saying there is no plan or order in the universe, and we are the victims of our circumstances. God does not want us to live like this. He is in absolute control of every single event in this life. He is the Master over the things that affect His purpose for each of us. When we face times of adversity, rather than minimize His ability and dominion, we should submit to Him and rejoice in the fact that He is watching over us with love and extreme care. Understanding this can do only one thing and that is to bring comfort as we face inevitable struggles.

SCRIPTURE IS CLEAR: THERE ARE NO COINCIDENCES WITH GOD.

I remember a particular time when I was struggling with discouragement, doubt, fear, and loneliness. I spent many evenings having long conversations with a close friend to whom I poured out my heart for hours. Many times during these talks, my friend stopped me and said, "Remember, God is in control." This statement became an anchor in my life. No matter how hard the winds blew or how much the adversity intensified, my soul remained anchored to the simple truth: God is in control. I discovered that when a person is able to face terrifying obstacles with the assurance of God's complete control, an awesome sense of power and assurance begins to well up inside his heart.

GOD WORKS *All Things for Good*

Behold, the eye of the LORD is on those who fear Him, On those who hope for His lovingkindness.... Our soul waits for the LORD; He is our help and our shield.

PSALM 33:18, 20

GOD IS IN CONTROL, and His Word underscores this truth. First, we find comfort in the fact that almighty God—who is in absolute control of everything—is intimately and continually involved in our individual lives every single day. God never stops providing for, protecting, watching over, or caring for each of us. Because He is sovereign and all-knowing, He knows exactly what we need for today and tomorrow.

Because God is sovereign, we have the assurance that He will work out every single circumstance in our lives for something good, no matter what. It may be painful, difficult, or seemingly impossible, but God can and will use that situation to achieve His divine purpose. Romans 8:28 makes this clear: "We know that God causes all things to work together for good to those who love God, to those who are called according to His purpose." This statement makes sense only when we realize that He is who He tells us He is—almighty God, infinite in wisdom.

God is our Protector. We have the assurance that nothing can touch us apart from His permissive will.

Psalm 34:7 explains, "The angel of the LORD encamps around those who fear Him, and rescues them." When something happens that is painful or unexplainable in our lives, does that mean God lost control for a moment? No, because we know that these things cannot happen unless He allows them. This hope enables us to go forward by faith believing that God will deal with every problem or challenge we encounter. He protects us, but He also allows us to face difficulty and even sorrow so that our faith is strengthened and hope emboldened.

NO MATTER WHAT PAIN, TRIAL, OR TRAGEDY COMES YOUR WAY, REJOICE THAT YOUR FATHER WILL BE THERE TO WORK IT OUT FOR YOUR GOOD.

My friend, when you begin to understand that God is in complete control of this world and everything in it, your life will change forever. God is sovereign. No matter what pain, trial, or tragedy comes your way, rejoice that your Father will be there to work it out for your good.

Tough TRAINING

Consider it all joy, my brethren, when you encounter various trials, knowing that the testing of your faith produces endurance. And let endurance have its perfect result, so that you may be perfect and complete, lacking in nothing.

JAMES 1:2–4

ADVERSITY IS ONE OF LIFE'S inescapable experiences, and not one of us is ever happy when it affects us personally. A popular theology says, "Just trust God and think rightly; then you won't have hardship." In searching Scripture, however, we see that God has advanced His greatest servants through adversity, not prosperity.

God isn't interested in building a generation of fainthearted Christians. Instead, He uses trials to train up stalwart, Spirit-filled soldiers for Jesus Christ. Sometimes, it is hard to hear about the trials our friends are facing. We enjoy times when there is no hint of sorrow or ill will. But we live in a fallen world, and if we live long enough, adversity will strike. We will battle feelings of discouragement. We may wonder, *Lord, what on earth are You doing?*

Hardship is a part of life; it can cause despair, sometimes to the point of disillusionment with Christianity. When we encounter such difficulty, we typically consider the ordeal unfair, unbelievable, and unbearable.

Our attitude is usually, "It's not fair, God." But we should be asking, "God, what is Your point of view?"

If our lives were free from persecution or trials—if we had everything we wanted and no problems—what would we know about our heavenly Father? Our view of Him would be unscriptural and most likely out of balance. Without adversity, we would never understand who God is or what He is like. How can God prove His faithfulness unless He allows some situations from which He must rescue us?

GOD USES TRIALS TO TRAIN UP STALWART, SPIRIT-FILLED SOLDIERS FOR JESUS CHRIST.

Do you want the kind of faith that is based *only* on what you have heard or read? It is never *your* truth until God works it into your life.

Adversity can be a deadly discouragement or God's greatest tool for advancing spiritual growth. Your response can make all the difference. Remember that God has a purpose for the hardship He's allowed, and it fits with His wonderful plan for your life.

God's Presence and PEACE

Cast all your anxiety on him because he cares for you.

1 PETER 5:7 NIV

SOMETIMES TRIALS pour an emotional, steady rain over our lives until we find ourselves saying, "Enough!"

We all face stress. The death of a loved one, an accident on the way home from school or work, or the loss of a close relationship can leave us struggling with feelings of hopelessness, doubt, and confusion. But God has a solution for our tensions and pressures. He knows our longing for peace and safety, and He has promised to provide both for us.

One of the ways Jesus dealt with the pressures of life was by stepping away from the furious pace of His world to be alone with the Father. He understood that communion with God was essential to maintaining His relationship with the Father.

When we go to God in prayer, we express our needs and total dependence on Him. The psalmist wrote, "Cast your burden upon the LORD and He will sustain you; He will never allow the righteous to be shaken" (Psalm 55:22). The idea of casting or rolling our burden onto the Lord is that we acknowledge Him as our sufficiency.

He is our Burden-Bearer, and He can carry the weight that accompanies a stressful situation.

Why do some people struggle in prayer? Many think that because they have sinned against God in the past, He won't hear their prayers. God wants us to know that He is waiting for us to come to Him, just as the father waited for the prodigal son (Luke 15:20). When we go to God in prayer, we find that He receives us with unconditional love and forgiveness.

HE IS OUR BURDEN-BEARER, AND HE CAN CARRY THE WEIGHT THAT ACCOMPANIES A STRESSFUL SITUATION.

God knows your need for peace even before you ask. And He never grows tired of hearing you pray and asking for His wisdom, guidance, and protection. Never hesitate to take your problems to God. Whenever there is failure of any kind, be sure to take action with God through prayer immediately. Confess your sin and where you got off track. Ask Him to restore your fellowship with Him and then make a commitment to live your life under the protective shadow of His purity.

CHAPTER EIGHT

PRAYER: *It's War on the Floor*

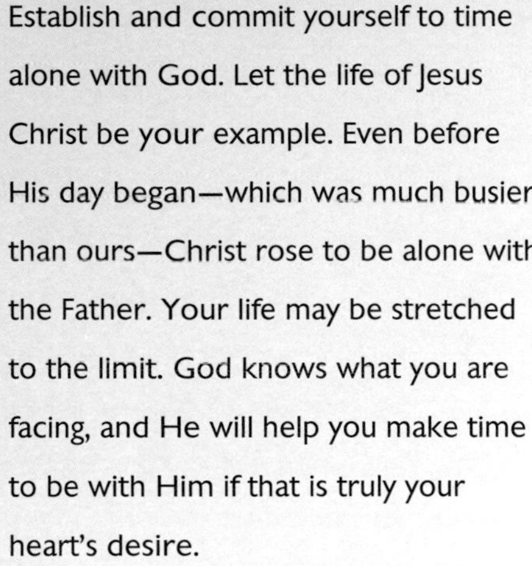

Establish and commit yourself to time alone with God. Let the life of Jesus Christ be your example. Even before His day began—which was much busier than ours—Christ rose to be alone with the Father. Your life may be stretched to the limit. God knows what you are facing, and He will help you make time to be with Him if that is truly your heart's desire.

TENACIOUS *Prayer*

Ask, and it will be given to you; seek, and you will find; knock, and it will be opened to you. For everyone who asks receives, and he who seeks finds, and to him who knocks it will be opened.

MATTHEW 7:7–8

SOMETIMES WELL-MEANING CHRISTIANS miss fantastic opportunities and blessings, all because they have taken a completely passive role in their prayer lives. Too often, the seeking and knocking described in Matthew 7:7–11 are overlooked as the believer merely asks God for something once or twice and then sits back and forgets all about the matter.

For example, when you begin making college plans, what would happen if you simply sat on the couch and said, "Lord, please show me exactly where You want me to go to college"? Now, on the surface, this seems to be the best way to start the process. But what if you never got off the couch? Instead of talking with other students, visiting campuses, ordering catalogs, reviewing school Web sites, and meeting with counselors, you simply sat and waited for an answer from the Lord. Most likely you would still be sitting there when classes started the next fall!

Or think about someone who honestly desires a deeper understanding of Scripture, sets his Bible down on the table, and prays, "Lord, please open up the truths of Your Word to me. I desperately want to understand Your Word." That person can pray continuously, but the only way for him to get a deeper understanding of the Bible would not be simply by asking, but also by digging into the Word for himself.

What about matters of spiritual warfare? How should a Christian pray when he is under attack? Do two-sentence platitudes work then? If you ever hope to defeat your spiritual enemy—and you have a very real enemy—you must begin with active, intentional prayer.

IF YOU EVER HOPE TO DEFEAT YOUR SPIRITUAL ENEMY— AND YOU HAVE A VERY REAL ENEMY— YOU MUST BEGIN WITH ACTIVE, INTENTIONAL PRAYER.

Always PERSEVERE!

With all prayer and petition pray at all times in the Spirit, and with this in view, be on the alert with all perseverance and petition for all the saints.

EPHESIANS 6:18

WHEN YOU PRAY, do you have confidence that God will answer, or do you feel unworthy of His attention? Are your prayers specific or general? Is your prayer life a haphazard response to needs and desires, or nourishment for the life of Jesus Christ within you?

Prayer is not only asking and receiving, but also thanking, adoring, and praising the Lord God. There are two responsibilities in prayer—God's responsibility and our responsibility. You cannot have one without the other; prayer is both divine and human. We are to become actively involved in the prayer process. Prayer is not a spectator sport!

Every request, every desire of our hearts, and every need should begin with prayer—asking God for permission and seeking to know His will. Because Jesus Christ has come into our lives and because He has now become our Life, we have the privilege and authority to approach Him and make a request (Ephesians 3:11–12; Hebrews 4:16).

There is a vital element in prayer that most people overlook, which is *steadfastness* in prayer. We may not see anything happening, but a delay between our asking and our receiving doesn't mean that God isn't going to answer our prayers. He may delay answering prayer requests, even if your request is, in fact, in line with His will. Why does He do this? If He sees within us wrong motives, attitudes of rebellion, bitterness, or unforgiveness, or if He notices certain unhealthy habits in our lifestyles, God postpones the answer for His children. He already may have it packaged and ready to send your way, but He cannot and will not do so until you are in a spiritual position to receive it.

God's timing is perfect. It may not match our own, but you can be sure that it will match His will for our lives. He is far more interested in our knowing Him than our getting from Him everything our hearts desire. We cannot lose heart in prayer. When we persist, we gain new insight into the heart of God and reap rewards far greater than merely an instantly fulfilled request.

WE ARE TO BECOME ACTIVELY INVOLVED IN THE PRAYER PROCESS. PRAYER IS NOT A SPECTATOR SPORT!

Make Prayer a PRIORITY

Therefore let us draw near with confidence to the throne of grace, so that we may receive mercy and find grace to help in time of need.

HEBREWS 4:16

WOULD YOU SAY THAT PRAYER is a vital part of your daily schedule? There is no way for Jesus Christ to be a part of my life unless I am praying. I talk, share, and relate with Him all day long. He is my Life!

I know Christians who have allowed activities to encroach on their lives to a point where prayer is shifted to a lesser level. They may diligently serve the Lord, but they are doing this in their own strength and limited wisdom. One of the primary reasons we fail to pray is because we busy ourselves with distractions and don't think we have time to do what is most important.

Why do people do this? I'm convinced it's a matter of denial and avoidance. We deny our need for God. We think by working overtime, we will gain favor with Him, but all we are doing is draining our lives of His strength.

Nowhere does the Bible say that prayer is easy. It often involves a struggle. There may even be times when Satan will attack you as you are on your knees, harassing you with doubt and sending distracting thoughts into your mind. One of Satan's most effective weapons is discouragement. He wants to tempt you to have feelings of worthlessness before God. Scripture shatters this fear by boldly proclaiming that you and I have freedom in Christ to approach the very throne of God in prayer. You are His beloved child—endowed with His goodness and declared not guilty because of His death on Calvary's cross. When you go to the Lord, do not be meek and embarrassed; instead, bow before Him and rejoice!

God listens to your requests and wants you to know that nothing is too small or too large for Him. He tells us that when we ask, seek, knock, and trust Him, He will answer and give us His best. This means that many times He will give you what you are requesting. But if He says no or wait, you can be sure that He has something much better in mind.

If you will actively apply these simple truths to your situations, God will transform your prayer life. Once you establish a prayer time with Him, you will begin to harness His strength to fight your spiritual battles. And when you fight your battles on your knees, you'll win every time!

WHEN YOU GO TO THE LORD, DO NOT BE MEEK AND EMBARRASSED; INSTEAD, BOW BEFORE HIM AND REJOICE!

THE ARMOR *of Prayer*

For our struggle is not against flesh and blood, but against the rulers, against the powers, against the world forces of this darkness, against the spiritual forces of wickedness in the heavenly places.

EPHESIANS 6:12

HAVE YOU EVER FACED CIRCUMSTANCES so overwhelming that you wondered how you would stand up under them? More than likely, there will come a time when you will have to stand up for what you believe about God—in college, in graduate school, or in life. And though you may experience feelings of spiritual weakness, God will give you the strength and the wisdom to be concise about your faith. You don't have to feel fearful or weak. Ask Him to give you the right words to say when others ask you about your Christian faith.

Though none of us enjoy times of feeling vulnerable, they do not have to be negative experiences. If our weakness results in self-pity, despair, or sin, then it is harmful; but if it drives us to dependency upon God, it is beneficial. Oftentimes fear and discouragement are caused by satanic attack—a willful, determined assault by the devil for the purpose of harming your spirit, soul, or body.

The Bible tells us to stand firm and resist the devil (Ephesians 6:11, James 4:7).

There is only one way to stand and it is firmly planted on the Word of God. Notice in Scripture that Paul does not say, "Arm yourself and go fight the enemy." He does this for two reasons. First, the battle for our salvation already has been won at the cross. Once you are God's child, you are eternally secure—Satan cannot have your soul nor your eternal life (John 10:29–30).

Second, God is the one who fights for us. We can do nothing in our own strength. He empowers us to stand firm and to advance against the enemy. Satan's goal is to thwart the Lord's plan for you, and he can do a significant amount of damage. He is out to steal your peace and joy, cause confusion and anger, and encourage wrong relationships in your life. He will do anything he can to cheat you out of the blessings the Lord has promised. And the holier you attempt to live your life before God, the stronger the attacks are likely to be. Satan wants to ruin your witness and make sure that you are as ineffective as possible.

It is in times of prayer that God teaches you about Himself—His ways and how you should live your life.

THE ENEMY HAS NO DEFENSE AGAINST PERSEVERING PRAYER, WHICH CRUSHES HIS MIGHT AND SENDS HIM RUNNING.

He releases His energy, divine power, and protection, enabling us to live a godly, holy, and peaceful life—regardless of our circumstances.

It is only through prayer that our minds and spirits can discern what the average person cannot detect. Prayer is one way God can forewarn us of Satan's attacks, which may be aimed anywhere—our finances, relationships, or health. The one thing he hates above all else is the believer who knows how to persist in prayer and claim the promises of God. The enemy has no defense against persevering prayer, which crushes his might and sends him running.

for the Graduate

PUT ON *the Armor of God*

Therefore, take up the full armor of God, so that you will be able to resist in the evil day, and having done everything, to stand firm.

EPHESIANS 6:13

THOUGH AT TIMES—ESPECIALLY IN OUR PRESENT AGE—it seems we are in the midst of a horrendous physical battle, the real war is against the powers of spiritual darkness. Satan's goal has not changed over the years. The enemy knows his ultimate destiny, yet he will never give up his evil intent until Christ banishes him to the eternal lake of fire (Revelation 20:10). The only way he can do damage to the kingdom of God now is by enticing God's beloved children to yield to sin, thus damaging their fellowship with the Lord.

Satan will try to discourage you by filling your mind with an array of doubt and confusion, but you do not have to believe him. The message of the gospel of Christ is given to you as a sure authority. God's Word provides all the details you need to know about Satan.

Paul laid out the battle plan in the sixth chapter of Ephesians. First, we must identify the enemy (vv. 11–12); second, we are to dress in the full armor of God and stand firm (vv. 13–17). The next verse reveals the key to withstanding Satan's onslaughts—we must appropriate the strength of the living God. How do we get His power into our lives, to be unleashed in any and every circumstance? There is only one way: by prayer (v. 18).

Make a habit of claiming the armor of God each morning before you leave your house—this is a conscious act of submitting your life to the Lord as your final authority. Acknowledging your need for Him is a sign not of weakness, but of unshakable trust. When you place your faith in Jesus Christ, heaven is on your side.

WHEN YOU PLACE YOUR FAITH IN JESUS CHRIST, HEAVEN IS ON YOUR SIDE.

Whatever transpires in your life, the wisest decision you will ever make is the decision to spend time with the Lord on a regular basis. This teaches you to recognize Satan's movement and prepares you for battle when the enemy approaches. Paul told the Ephesians they were in a war, but clothed in the armor of God, they were assured of victory.

CHAPTER NINE

THE BIBLE: *The Sourcebook of Life*

The Bible is God's unfolding revelation of Himself. It is His Word to the human race, explaining His intervention in history and nature, and His arrival in this world as the God-man. The Word of God was given to us so that we might grow in our relationship with Him. It is our instruction book for life.

Think RIGHTLY

What you heard from me, keep as the pattern of sound teaching, with faith and love in Christ Jesus.

2 TIMOTHY 1:13 NIV

OUR BELIEF SYSTEM GOVERNS OUR LIFESTYLE AND CHOICES—it is the foundation from which we form our opinions and make decisions. For Christians, it is absolutely essential to know what we believe and why. Most people inherit their convictions from their parents and simply absorb those ideas without really investigating them.

But to be certain our system of thinking is accurate, we must base it on the Word of God and not on habit, culture, or even family heritage. A belief system is like a mental grid through which all outside information must pass. If our mental grid has been built on the truth of the Bible, then we can detect false doctrine and philosophy.

False doctrine is usually mixed up with just enough truth to make it sound good. Many Christians who are not grounded in their faith are easily led astray by doctrines that are genuinely too good to be true. They eagerly support an agenda that is inconsistent with

God's Word because it offers license to live according to one's fleshly desires (2 Timothy 4:3).

Believers should know their convictions so that they can present those beliefs convincingly to others. While it is the work of the Holy Spirit to bring the lost to Christ, God may choose to use us to instruct unbelievers in the way of truth. Our world is full of people who are desperate, lonely, and hurting. They yearn for the amazing hope that we have. But they desire hope sourced in truth, not on someone else's opinion.

There is no question that our society is permeated with godless ideas and philosophies that can ultimately destroy us. But if our belief system is based upon Scripture, we will recognize deceitful teaching when we hear it and will address real needs with real answers.

IF OUR BELIEF SYSTEM IS BASED UPON SCRIPTURE, WE WILL RECOGNIZE DECEITFUL TEACHING WHEN WE HEAR IT AND WILL ADDRESS REAL NEEDS WITH REAL ANSWERS.

THE ETERNAL, *Timeless Truth*

Sanctify Christ as Lord in your hearts, always being ready to make a defense to everyone who asks you to give an account for the hope that is in you, yet with gentleness and reverence.

1 PETER 3:15

PEOPLE OFTEN HAVE DIFFICULTY expressing what they believe. Instead of having a verifiable belief system based on godly principles, too many Christians embrace a few vague ideas. Peter told us always to be ready to give a reason for what we believe (1 Peter 3:15). So we want to be sure that we correctly understand scriptural truth. Let's consider a list of absolute truths that should be a foundational part of your belief system.

- *The Bible.* In keeping with 2 Timothy 3:16, we refer to Scripture as the inspired Word of God, or as "God-breathed," which means the Lord chose individuals to record what He spoke to them. The Word of the living God was given to us so that we might grow in our relationship with Him. This is our instruction book for life and the final authority for what we believe.
- *The Godhead.* The truth of the triune God appears throughout the Bible. Our one God consists of three distinct persons: God the Father, God the Son, and God the Holy Spirit. They are characterized by the

same attributes—they are eternal, omnipotent, omniscient, and immutable—but each person has a different function.

- *Satan.* The Bible tells us that Satan is real. He so desired to be like God that he rebelled against the Creator, who subsequently cast him and his co-conspirators to earth. As the source of all sin, he instigates pain, sorrow, and spiritual death. As Christians, however, we have no cause to fear Satan. We are under the protection of the Holy Spirit. In addition, all of us who have read Scripture have seen Satan's obituary. It is in Revelation 20, where he is thrown into a lake of fire, eternally punished for his rebellion toward almighty God (v. 10).
- *Man.* God created man in His image in order to love us and fellowship with us. But when Adam and Eve disobeyed God, man's relationship to the Creator changed. At the same time, man's very nature became corrupt so that each of us is born with our will inclined away

WE OWN THE MOST PRECIOUS BOOK ON THE FACE OF THE EARTH. IF WE KNOW WHAT IT SAYS, WE WILL KNOW WHAT WE MUST BELIEVE TO LIVE FOR HIS GLORY.

from God. No man can earn God's forgiveness or acceptance. But redemption works in our lives to change our nature and bend it back toward God.

- *Salvation.* The simplest definition of *salvation* is "the gift of God's grace, whereby He provides forgiveness for our sins." Jesus Christ died on a cross as a substitute for us. That is, at the time of the Savior's death, God the Father placed all the sin of mankind upon Him. So our sin-debt was paid in absolute fullness. Now we are sealed in the Holy Spirit and eternally secure.
- *The Church.* The church is the whole body of Christ —believers from every part of the globe. If you have

trusted Jesus Christ as your personal Savior, you are in the body of Christ, and God is your heavenly Father. As followers of Jesus, we are to express love for one another—encouraging, helping, and praying for fellow Christians. Our conduct should be in keeping with the One we call Lord and Master of our lives.

Every one of these issues is a vital part of the Christian's belief system, and they are all found in one place—the Word of God. As His children, we own the most precious book on the face of the earth. If we know what it says, we will know what we must believe to live for His glory.

Tune in to Hear GOD'S WILL

Then you will call upon Me and come and pray to Me, and I will listen to you. You will seek Me and find Me when you search for Me with all your heart.

JEREMIAH 29:12–13

PEOPLE USE ALL KINDS OF METHODS to make decisions. Far too many Christians choose to say, "Lord, this is what I'm going to do. If this doesn't suit You, You just let me know." That is no way to find out what God wants you to do.

Having the spiritual discernment to make wise decisions is critical. It is an asset that is not acquired instantly, but grows out of a life totally consecrated to and dependent upon God. When you seek godly discernment with all your heart and your motives are pure, He will help you make wise decisions. He knows your heart, and He wants you to do the right thing.

In seeking God for perfect guidance, you must first confess your sins and allow God complete access to your mind and will. When your relationship with Jesus Christ is right, He will give you the wisdom you need at every turn in life.

Are you afraid to make decisions? Do you vacillate between two paths because you can't determine which way to turn? Sometimes this is due to a self-image

problem. You may have a hard time trusting yourself, and you fear the consequences of making the wrong decision. Other times it is the result of sin that blocks your communication with God. How can you know what God wants you to do if your conscience is not clear?

A guilty conscience is to the mind what static is to a radio. You hear two voices that say different things. When you struggle between your will and God's will, you don't get a clear message. There is instead a distorted, fractional sound. Your mind and will are divided, and you cannot know what God is saying.

It's time to turn the dial to God's frequency and tune in to His message for your life. When you do, He will give you the discernment and wisdom required for godly living.

DISCERNMENT IS AN ASSET THAT IS NOT ACQUIRED INSTANTLY, BUT GROWS OUT OF A LIFE TOTALLY CONSECRATED TO AND DEPENDENT UPON GOD.

God's Instruction MANUAL

> *"The Helper, the Holy Spirit, whom the Father will send in My name, He will teach you all things, and bring to your remembrance all that I said to you."*
>
> JOHN 14:26

LIFE IS COMPOSED OF ONE DECISION AFTER ANOTHER. Some of them are minor decisions and some are major, but all require godly discernment. You may be facing a decision about where to go to college or where to look for work. You may be asking God what you should do. Maybe you're trying to make a decision about a potential spouse. You're not sure whether it's the Lord's will for you to be married or not. Perhaps you're a student and you're trying to choose a major for your college career, and you just can't seem to get God's clear direction about it.

Whatever decision you are facing, one thing is certain: God is always willing to show you His will, His plan, and His purpose. He always desires to give you guidance and direction in your decisions. God spoke to Abraham, saying, "Go forth from your country, and from your relatives and from your father's house, to the land which I will show you" (Genesis 12:1). He spoke to Gideon and told him to lead the people of God against those who had enslaved them (Judges 6:14). He sent an angel to

Mary to tell her of the Christ child (Luke 1:28–31). When Paul was headed in one direction to preach the gospel, the Holy Spirit said to him, "Paul, that's not My will for your life at this time" (Acts 16:6–7).

Has the Lord ceased speaking to men and women today, as He did in biblical times? Absolutely not! God has spoken in many ways, recorded in the Old and New Testaments, and He continues to speak to people today. His method of speaking may have changed, but the fact that He speaks and gives us direction for our lives has not.

The Word of God is His clear instruction as to how you should live—the basis upon which you should make decisions. God has given you Scripture for guidance and instruction. He also has given you the Holy Spirit, who indwells in you to interpret the Word so that from the Word and through His Spirit, you can have assurance.

HIS METHOD OF SPEAKING MAY HAVE CHANGED, BUT THE FACT THAT HE SPEAKS AND GIVES US DIRECTION FOR OUR LIVES HAS NOT.

GOD'S GUIDANCE
—*in Everything*

I have directed you
in the way of
wisdom;
I have led you in
upright paths.
When you walk,
your steps will not be
impeded;
And if you run, you
will not stumble.

PROVERBS 4:11–12

HAVE YOU EVER THOUGHT ABOUT how interested God is in your daily affairs—those little, insignificant things that don't seem to make a difference to most people? Christians often separate the spiritual life from the common, everyday life. But God never intended that to be the approach you take. He intends to be involved in every decision you make, no matter how small.

If you want to make wise decisions, you must live a consecrated life. This means you must walk committed to Him. Every morning surrender your life to Him. Separate yourself to Him, for Him, and under Him for that day. Paul said, "I urge you, brethren, by the mercies of God, to present your bodies as a living and holy sacrifice, acceptable to God, which is your spiritual service of worship. And do not be conformed to this world, but be transformed by the renewing of your mind, so that you may prove what the will of God is, that which is good and acceptable and perfect" (Romans 12:1–2).

Every believer can walk in confidence and assurance that he is walking in God's will. If you persist in prayer, lean on His promises, and wait for His peace, He will speak truth to your heart and mind. Isaiah 30:21 states, "Your ears will hear a word behind you, 'This is the way, walk in it,' whenever you turn to the right or to the left."

IF YOU WILL LISTEN CAREFULLY, HE WILL WHISPER TO YOU VERY QUIETLY, *MY CHILD, THIS IS THE WAY. WALK IN IT.*

This is a beautiful example of how the Lord speaks to our hearts. Day by day, I have to ask, "Lord, what next?" And I have to hear Him say, *This is the way. Walk in it.* I hear that many times during the day. The Lord will say the same thing to you. If you are committed to Jesus Christ—if He is your Savior, your Master, your Lord—and it is your heart's desire to follow Him, you will find a confidence in your spiritual life that you have never known before. If you will listen carefully, He will whisper to you very quietly, *My child, this is the way. Walk in it.*

The Pursuit of WISDOM

Buy the truth and do not sell it; get wisdom, discipline and understanding.

PROVERBS 23:23 NIV

THE WRITER OF PROVERBS REMINDED US that "Wisdom is supreme; therefore get wisdom. Though it cost all you have, get understanding" (Proverbs 4:7 NIV). So how do we gain the wisdom of God for our lives?

We gain wisdom when we seek God. We must believe, as James instructed us, that if we go to God with even the smallest detail, He will hear our prayer and answer it. This is exactly what He does.

We gain wisdom when we learn to meditate on God's Word. Scripture provides a solution for every problem or decision we face. We can trust the Word of God to provide the guidance we need.

We gain wisdom when we learn to obey the principles of Scripture. Before David could rule as king, he had to learn to obey God. He also had to learn to follow the pathway God placed before him. This meant that he submitted his human desires to God. Do you love the Lord so much that you are willing to release all that you have so God can live His life through you?

We gain wisdom as a result of prayer. In times of prayer, we learn to humble our hearts before God. We also learn to be quiet and listen for God's voice through the Holy Spirit who lives within each believer.

We gain wisdom by observing how God works in our world. At times, the workings of the world may seem out of control. However, always remember that He is sovereign. He is never out of control.

We gain wisdom through wise counsel. Talk over your problems with trusted Christian friends, a counselor, or a pastor. Once they have given you their view or counsel, take this to God in prayer. If what they have told you is from God, it will not violate Scripture.

We seek wisdom to please God and to gain His perspective on our lives and individual situations. Faith and trust are necessary in gaining the wisdom of God. Human reasoning will fail you. Only the wisdom of God will guide you safely through life.

HUMAN REASONING WILL FAIL YOU. ONLY THE WISDOM OF GOD WILL GUIDE YOU SAFELY THROUGH LIFE.

AFTERWORD: *Lay a Solid Foundation*

YOU CAN LAY A STRONG FOUNDATION FOR YOUR LIFE by asking God to come to you and, if you have never accepted His Son as your Savior, asking Him to come into your heart and forgive your sins. Realize the moment you do this, you are a child of God—a new creature in Christ—and you no longer stand at a distance from God. You belong to Him, and His eternal reward and blessing are yours to enjoy and experience from now until forever.

If you have drifted in your devotion to the Savior and feel as though each day you live you grow more distant in your relationship to God, then pray that He would draw you near to Himself. He knows your weaknesses, and if you will tell Him that you no longer want to be in charge of your life, He will come to you in a mighty way and bring hope and light to your dark and hopeless situation (Isaiah 55:6–9).

These simple acts of prayer are powerful. Tell God that you want your life to be His. Commit your desires, hopes, and dreams to Him, and you will be amazed at the way He works everything together for your good and His glory.

Also Available from Dr. Stanley!

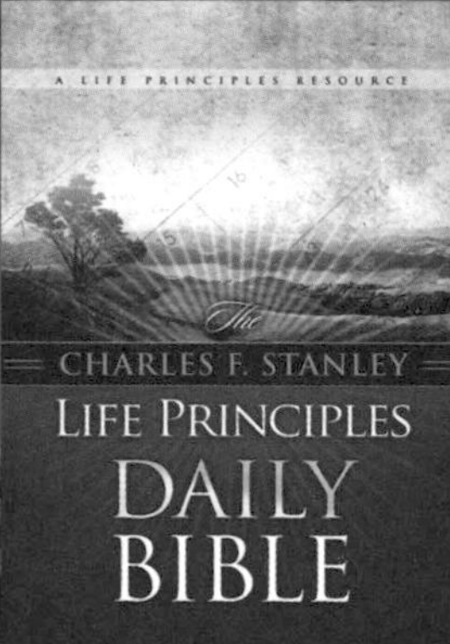

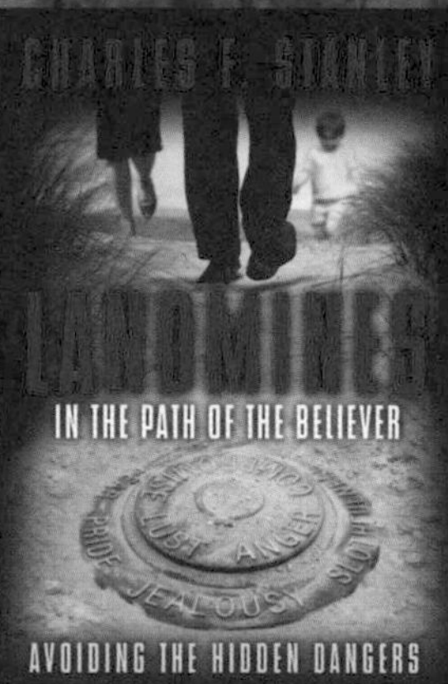

The *Life Principles Daily Bible* provides 365 daily readings from the Old Testament, New Testament, Psalms, and Proverbs; accompanied by Dr. Stanley's notes and lessons.

Dr. Stanley identifies ten destructive temptations and gives Christians the hope and skills they need to live an abundant and obedient life.

Stay Connected...

Dr. Stanley and In Touch Ministries are just a click away. Find exactly what you need faster and easier than ever before at www.intouch.org.